HOPE
FOR THE
BROKEN

by
JORGE LUÍS

Published by:
Creative Press
P.O. Box 769000
Dallas, TX. 75376-9000

Copyright © 2015

ISBN#978-0-89985-531-8

All rights reserved under International Copyright Law. Written permission must be secured from the publisher to use or reproduce any part of this book.

All Scripture quotations, unless otherwise indicated, are noted NIV, from the Holy Bible, New International Version. (NIV). Copyright © 1973, 1978, 1984, International Bible Society. Used by permission of Zondervan Publishing House. All rights reserved.

All Scriptures noted NKJV are taken from the New King James Version. Copyright © 1979, 1980, 1982 by Thomas Nelson, Inc. Used by permission. All rights reserved.

Cover Design: Sabrina Rosamilia

ACKNOWLEDGMENTS

I want to thank everyone who helped me to make it possible for this book to be published. In addition, I want to thank all who prayed for us, and Ms. Polly Harder, who was sensitive to the voice of the Holy Spirit, and gave us the chance to publish this book. It was Ms. Harder who instructed us to add the final chapter in this edition, so I could describe some of God's miracles that were done in and through our lives in Brazil.

Finally, I want to thank Leia Guerra, Emanuelle and Frederico Maciel for their dedication in translating this book into English, and all the others I may have forgotten to mention, but who will certainly be rewarded by God, according to His riches and glory.

In the love of Christ Jesus.

PREFACE

Today, if you talk about a miracle, people know what you're talking about. You may even know of some people who have had a supernatural experience in your own life, whether it's physical, emotional or in the spiritual realm. In the scientific environment, much is said about the undeniable existence of God and a supernatural power that heals diseases. In fact, a Brazilian national magazine has brought a cover story entitled "Fé Cura" which means, Faith Healing. In the article it states that science itself has admitted that what the Scriptures have already shown us so long ago are true.

In the Book of Daniel, the Prophet Daniel foretold that knowledge would multiply in our day, which is undoubtedly being accomplished. However, God imposed limits to everything, including science. There are some diseases that still have no cure, which not only shows our human limitation, but science's limitation, as well. This is where the Divine action begins. Mankind's limits only show the unlimited power of God.

The triune God exercises His sovereignty over the universe and cares for each of us as the "apple of His eye." He loved the world so much that He sent His Son, so that anyone who believes in Him should not perish, but by the Holy Spirit, they will recognize they are sinners; they will repent and receive eternal life.

So whatever the miracle is that you need, just believe, because all things are possible to him who believes.

May you be richly blessed by reading this book.

Jorge Luís

TABLE OF CONTENTS

INTRODUCTION..9

Chapter 1
DEEP WOUNDS THAT MARKED MY LIFE......................13

Chapter 2
FOLLOWING MY OWN PATH..25

Chapter 3
WHERE WILL I GO FROM YOUR SPIRIT?......................43

Chapter 4
SEARCHING FOR HELP..53

Chapter 5
FIREPROOF..69

Chapter 6
THE GREAT WORK...83

Chapter 7
THE FULFILLMENT OF THE PROMISE..........................93

Chapter 8
THERE IS HOPE FOR THE BROKEN..................................117

Chapter 9
FINAL WORDS..119

INTRODUCTION

"He lifted me out of the slimy pit, out of the mud and mire; he set my feet on a rock and gave me a firm place to stand" (Psalm 40:2).

Exactly what this verse states is what I saw happen in Jorge's life. And today, with immense pleasure and joy, I can say that I have witnessed this miracle of what the Lord has done in this man.

Who can frustrate God's plans for a life that is precious to Him and who is chosen from his mother's womb? May God be praised! I know that nothing can undo the designs of the heart of a God, who loves us unconditionally, with immeasurable and indescribable love.

The Lord gave me the opportunity to meet Jorge Luís. In His mercy, the Holy Spirit of God gave me a word that was against the situation he lived in at that moment. Since then, I followed a long history, in regards to his transformation in facing a delicate and adverse situation. Human opinion would have said that Jorge would be considered to be someone who was born to "go wrong." A despicable and worthless person. But the Word says that, "He (God) raises the poor out of the dust …" (Psalm 113:7, NKJV).

This is exactly what He did for Jorge. He designed Jorge to "go right," and in order to achieve this, God did not give up on him at any time during this amazing transformation. God had set him apart, before the beginning of time, and God has preserved him from both spiritual and physical death.

God, by His foreknowledge, had already decided to straighten all the rugged and tortuous paths of Jorge's life. He rescued him from the enemy and carried him into His wonderful light. Today, Jorge can witness about the wonders he has experienced in his own life through the powerful action of a God, Who has no limits to operate because His power does not depend on human capacity. We also know that this God neither slumbers nor sleeps, and all the time, was working to deliver this man. Glory to God!

The Lord turned this miserable person, Jorge, into a prince. He was stripped of his clothes that were stained by sin, and instead, he was given festive garments, representing a hope and a future. All of his past, pain, fear, wounds, tears, rejection, failure, disappointment, anguish, depression, frustration, and low self-esteem were nailed to the cross of Christ, all of which transformed him into a new creature. Now, he can be called a child of God and can become a living witness of a God, Who heals, saves and delivers.

Today, Jorge is aware of his physical body that once was enslaved by all kinds of lusts and abominations, but now carries the marks of the God Who redeemed him. Jorge knows the way. Even though it's a straight path, he has resigned himself to whatever sacrifices are necessary because God has given him an abundant life, guided by the sweet Spirit of God. Jorge is no longer dominated by sin, but assumes the posture of a new man, a new creation that the Word promises us we will be, once we accept Christ. Jorge knows that this is the path that will lead him to eternal life.

For you, reader, who is perhaps living in a similar situation that was once experienced by Jorge, I leave this message—There is an Almighty God, Who loves you and yearns to do something supernatural in your life. Just invite The King of Glory, Jesus Christ, to enter and to dwell in your heart. All things are possible to him who believes and nothing is too hard for God.

Remember, this portion is not just for Jorge, but also for all who want to be touched and transformed by this wonderful God, Who continually stands at the door and knocks.

Jorge, be faithful until death, yours is the crown of eternal life. I love you in Christ!

Reader, receive this book as a testimony of the power of God.

Aritânia

Chapter 1

DEEP WOUNDS THAT MARKED MY LIFE

"Your eyes saw my unformed body; all the days ordained for me were written in your book before one of them came to be" (Psalm 139:16).

"No, in all these things we are more than conquerors through him who loved us" (Romans 8:37).

Even though it is difficult to fully comprehend the depth of this verse, it assures us that regardless of our circumstances, we will have the victory in Him because of how great His love is for us.

At the time of our conception, there is only one chance that fertilization happens, and from that, life begins. But it is only the beginning. Unfortunately, many babies are aborted by a desperate mother, who is trying to get rid of an unwanted pregnancy—perhaps the result of a rape or union with a man who left her. Still, for those of us who are here, we have managed to overcome the obstacles. We've gone through the pregnancy period and are finally born. However, even before all this happened, God planned our existence and a future for each one of us.

I was born in Ilhéus, the countryside of Bahia, a city that has become known as the backdrop for very famous literary works. My mother, a sixteen year old, was the housemaid to a very rich man, but she became involved with his boss and got pregnant. Because she didn't want to cause a scandal or bring shame to the family, she could no longer stay on the job.

She was a pretty, young girl, and it was not hard to get a mate. However, as was expected, he soon informed her that even though he would take care of her, he would not take care of the child. No one knows for sure the reasons that led to his decision, but she accepted his condition. Thus, I was born—a beautiful and healthy boy. However, now she had to find someone who could raise me.

My mother went out through the city, door to door, offering me to anyone who would take me. Some of the people she spoke to said they were no longer of an age to raise a small child. Others wanted a girl because they already had many boys. That is until they fulfill what is written in Psalm 68:6,

"God sets the lonely in families, ..."

So, when she passed by Carneiro da Rocha Street, which is downtown, there was great excitement. What she was trying to do had spread among the neighbors, and everyone wanted to see the baby.

At this location, there lived a widow. When her daughter saw me, she was given a supernatural love for me. She fervently wanted to adopt me. Lia was 19 years old, and like other girls her age, she really liked to party. But after several attempts, appeals and promises that she would stop dating and leave the parties in order to take care of me, her mother allowed her to adopt me.

Immediately, she went looking for my mother, and found her across town. When she saw her, she yelled, "Hey, you! Lady! Bring the baby. My mom will raise him."

How faithful is God! No one can stop His plans for us. The Word says in John 10:10, that "The thief comes only to steal and kill and destroy; ..." But the Word also says,

"The reason the Son of God appeared was to destroy the devil's work" (1 John 3:8).

I can't say for sure, but I imagine how many times my mother possibly heard from others to just throw me in the trash or under a car. BUT GOD had a better plan, and He was already executing it for my life.

Now, I had a family that had come to love me as a son, without any distinction, but other complications began to appear. I started to have respiratory difficulties and very severe asthma attacks, which alarmed everyone. Home remedies weren't working anymore. Many times I was taken to the doctor's house, so he could save my life.

I went through many crises, but God, in His great love, delivered me from them all. Hallelujah! The keys of death and hell are in the hands of Jesus.

"And we know that in all things God works for the

good of those who love him, who have been called according to his purpose" (Romans 8:28).

This is what God's Word says, and it is true. It never returns empty or void, but rather, He does whatever He pleases. There were many places my mother walked, looking for a family who wanted to adopt me. However, before the foundation of the world, God had already prepared a place for me. Next to the family who adopted me, lived a woman. She was a servant of God. Her name is Sister Noemi Lopes. She was and still is a person who is admired by all. Her life represents a deep and authentic relationship with God.

Sister Lopes was a very wise woman, and every Sunday she invited that widow's daughters to go to church and attend Sunday school. Even though I was still very young, I was taken to the Baptist Church of Ilhéus, where I began to be taught the things of God. There, I heard my first Bible stories and learned the first songs that I kept in my heart for my whole life. I also learned about the death of Jesus, His forgiveness for my sins and the power of Christ's blood to wash all the filth of sin away.

From the beginning, God had set out a plan to rescue me. Despite the fact that my foster family did not have any biblical information to give me but He put Sister Noemi by my side to cover such a need. She knew how important it was and practiced what it says in Proverbs 22:6,

"Start children off on the way they should go, and even when they are old they will not turn from it."

Five years after she welcomed me, my foster grandmother was affected by cancer. She suffered a lot, despite all the attempts of the family to help her. Nothing could be done; she would only have a few months to live. I remember when I visited her at the hospital; she sat up to see me, but then quarreled with her daughter for bringing me there. She was a simple woman, who suffered, but she had a good heart. She received me as a son. She didn't know the severity of her illness. What she feared the most was not leaving her three daughters—it was leaving me. I was just a kid. Not long after, she passed away. Now we were alone.

It has been scientifically proven that in some cases, cancer is caused by "soul," our mind, will, and emotions, diseases—emotions like anguish and unforgiveness. We also know that God allows such events so that the soul of mankind can reach a level of brokenness and come to a place where it will totally surrender to Christ.

I'm not sure if my grandmother was saved or not. Only God, the Eternal Judge, can answer this question. However, I believe that the Holy Spirit is the only One Who raises awareness to mankind's sin, righteousness and judgment. He may have spoken to her heart, even in the last seconds of her life, leading her to Christ.

With the death of my grandmother, her daughters took care of me. I ended up with three mothers. Lia, the eldest, was very lovely; she was the one who was really responsible for me. I called her, "mother." Iracy was also very kind, unlike Vera, who was rigid. Vera disciplined me whenever necessary and kept me on a tight leash.

At six years old, I had a father, and later, brothers because my foster mother had married, and they had their own children. However, unlike Aunt Vera, my parents left me very much to myself. They did not have much control over what I was doing, where I was going, or who I was with. This lack of attention contributed to a very traumatic event in my life. At the age of ten, during a retreat, I was sexually abused by a seminary student. Afterward, I tried to talk with some people about what had happened, but since he was older than I was, nobody believed me. They just saw me as a child.

Psychology says that only 30 percent of an individual's personality is formed by genetic inheritance. The other 70 percent is the reflection of the environment they live in. So parents should pay close attention to the people their children are related to, as it states in 1 Corinthians 15:33,

> "Do not be misled: 'Bad company corrupts good character.'"

In the same way, the Bible advises parents to,
> "Start children off on the way they should go, and even when they are old they will not turn from it." (Proverbs 22:6).

The sexual abuse only added to all the other tough circumstances I had already experienced. This was the means that the devil used to try to destroy me for good. From then on, I began to have a conflict with religion, the church, and religious leaders. I thought it was all a lie.

A few years later, my adoptive parents began to face marital problems. My father had started to be unfaithful to my mother and was seeing other women. Their relationship became more difficult each day. Finally, needing an excuse to leave and go live with another family, my father began to pick on me. He demanded that my mother make a choice between him or me. Since she already had six biological children with him, she chose to send me to her sister's house.

Once again, I was now the outsider of a relationship. When I turned sixteen, I suffered another difficult and painful loss. I had to move away from everyone I loved. I moved in with my Aunt Vera, who had married and moved to Aracaju. She had also become a servant of God and a praying woman. She has continued to intercede for all of us.

At this time, my heart was already too hurt; I was traumatized and had no more family to call my own. This was all the devil wanted to create in my life, completely destroying any future expectation of ever having a home.

Separated from my mother and brothers, I looked for a way to reverse the situation. I wished to return to live near them and there was only one way to make that happen. I could study in a boarding school in EMARC Technique in Uruçuca, which was twenty-nine miles from Ilhéus.

I did the test and was classified to study Food Technology—a difficult course, which lasted two years, but that would give me the opportunity to fulfill my future.

When I arrived at the school the first day, it was unforgettable.

I needed to be there a day earlier, on Sunday, and that night there was nothing to eat. My mother only had money for a one-way ticket, and I did not have enough to buy food, so I ate some coconut cookies.

During the two years I was at school, I was not able to spend the weekends with my family. I knew that my adoptive father did not accept my presence. Instead, I spent it with some of my friends. Yet, in the midst of so many struggles and difficulties, I managed to graduate on time. I didn't celebrate with those who I graduated with because at the time, I was working on the entrance exam for another University. I was going to take another course on Food Engineering in João Pessoa, Paraíba. I passed, and I moved there. I lived in a room behind the house of a family who were friends of my aunt.

It was a very difficult time, and the money I had could barely sustain me. I could not go home for lunch, so my lunch was just a cup of sugarcane juice. I could only eat at night. Once, one of my aunts sent me a pair of scissors. She thought I could work and gain extra money as a hairdresser. Along with the scissors, she had also sent me some money. At today's rate, this would have been about fifty dollars. But when I opened the package, I realized that the package had been vandalized. Someone had already taken the money out.

Some time later, there was a strike at the college that lasted for a few months. So I decided I would have to leave school at that time. My stay there was becoming harder, and I ended up dropping out of the class. My only option was to work as a hairdresser to try to improve my life.

We were created in the image and likeness of a triune God: Father, Son and Holy Spirit (1 John 5:7, 8). In the same way, we are also made up of three parts: spirit, soul, and body. Each one plays a role, which can be described as follows: the Spirit is the breath of life given to us by God. It is where we receive all that comes from the Holy Spirit. The body reflects our behavior, externalizes our attitudes, reflexes, tastes, skills and is the temple of God. The soul is what logs all our emotions from life—from the womb—it begins to receive and store messages of affection or rejection, pain and trauma.

During my life, many bad feelings were recorded in my soul: the rejection and abandonment of my parents, the anguish and uncertainty of my young, adoptive mother who decided to leave me in exchange for the security of a man, and many others. In the middle of so many conflicting situations, I received all this information in my soul, and I kept a record of it.

The marks were deep for me because from a very young age my family talked about the adoption—explaining the reasons for it. Many adopted children, who don't know the truth about their adoption or only hear about it through other people, become insurgents and rebel against their adoptive parents. However, with me, it was different. God Himself allowed everything to be brought to light and nothing was hidden.

The teenage years are an extremely important phase in an individual's life. These years become the scene of many external and internal changes that define one's personality. During that time of my life, a major conflict began to emerge within me. It was generated by my desires, attractions and thoughts, all, which caused me to flee from God's plan for me.

Every boy needs a father figure as a reference to develop his masculinity, as well as a girl needs a mother figure to set her standards. However, during my childhood, the father figure practically did not exist. There were no men in the family who raised me, only four women. Besides that, from a very early age I had suffered male rejection. My natural father didn't want me, and my adoptive father didn't want me. Every male had rejected me. All this was being stored in my soul, along with many other injuries, which resulted in serious character flaws.

At that time, in all the difficult moments of my life, I did not know we had a present Heavenly Father. I hadn't discovered my Supreme Father—Abba, Father!

These feelings of rejection could have driven me to use drugs or alcohol. I could have become a thief or acquired other bad behavior patterns. Satan has a constant project he is working on: hurt the image of God, which is mankind. However, the weapon the enemy had waiting for me was the world of homosexuality. We see how this happens according to the behavior described in Romans 1:25-27,

> "They exchanged the truth about God for a lie, and worshiped and served created things rather than the Creator—who is forever praised ... Because of this, God gave them over to shameful lusts ... In the same way the men also abandoned natural relations with women and were inflamed with lust for one another. Men committed shameful acts with other men, and received in themselves the

due penalty for their error."

I looked for help in several places, trying to solve my problems. Psychologists said, "I could be happy like this; just find someone like me, and we could be happy together." I had tried religion, even though the hopes were slim to none because the tool the devil used to hurt me through the sexual abuse had been a seminary student and future pastor. Many people who tried to help me faced the same difficulty. They just did not have the courage to take on the problem. So, all attempts were unsuccessful.

But there is hope for the broken. Hallelujah! I looked at all the human resources and knocked on many doors, but without any success. God used this to prove to me that in the future there would only be one solution to my problem—JESUS, THE DOOR TO VICTORY!

Since I could not find a way out, I began to blame God. If He was Sovereign, why didn't He prevent this from happening to me? Unfortunately, at that time, what I did not know was that the only culprit and agent in all of this was Satan.

Since there was no answer, or maybe I still could not discern the voice of God, I started to live a homosexual lifestyle. I believed in God and loved Jesus. I respected that all things came from Him, but I thought He had no solution for me. Now I know ... what is impossible for mankind, is possible for God.

"... 'Everything is possible for one who believes'" (Mark 9:23).

Chapter 2

FOLLOWING MY OWN PATH

"'For my thoughts are not your thoughts, neither are your ways my ways,' declares the LORD. As the heavens are higher than the earth, so are my ways higher than your ways and my thoughts than your thoughts'" (Isaiah 55:8, 9).

Due to a plague that spread around the cocoa plantations in the region, a strong economic crisis shook up Ilhéus city. This caused my family to move to Aracaju in search of better living conditions. Then, when I returned to Paraíba, my house was unoccupied; this allowed me to be able to start my beauty shop there. I wanted to improve my profession, so I started doing courses that were provided by the great cosmetic industries in São Paulo. Consequently, my clientele increased so greatly that my house became too small. I had to change my beauty shop location to a public gallery.

Then, one of my clients suggested that I go to work with her cousin, who was a hairdresser in New York City. This was the chance I had been waiting for a long to acquire. I thought this was going to bring me financial freedom. But, as the Bible says in Mark 8:36,

"What good is it for someone to gain the whole

Cont.

world, yet forfeit their soul?"

However, I could not see this actually happening. At this time, I was already living with a man in a homosexual relationship. All my friends just thought he was only a cousin. I didn't have a relationship with God then. Every day I lived a sinful life that kept me in bondage. I lived subject to the kingdom of darkness.

There are three factors that can drive God to do something in an individual's life:
1. Prayer
2. Time
3. Our Will

1. PRAYER:

Prayer is the key to victory in our lives. The Bible tells us about Elijah's prayer, when he asked God to manifest Himself. God answered and "... the fire of the Lord fell from heaven and consumed all of the altar." The prayer of a righteous person is powerful and effective. It shakes up hell's structure.

2. TIME:

There is a time that is determined by God to all things, but we may or may not decide to cooperate with Him and His specific timing. When the Hebrews left Egypt, the journey to the Promise Land should only have taken forty days. But because of the rebellion of the people, the time was extended to forty years.

3. **OUR WILL**:
If we do not wish to receive anything from God, then nothing can or will be done. He gave us free will, and we can choose how our future will be. We need to cry out before God, and He will then answer us.

Man's soul reflects all of his inner feelings or emotions. The Christian psychiatrist, Dr. Fábio Damasceno, describes this in one of his books:

> "Man's soul has a structure, areas that are apart of our soul such as: *emotion, intellect, volition* (will), *conscience, free will, conscious,* and *unconscious*."

Emotion

The emotional world is the one whereby surrounds the affection, the sensations of sadness, wellbeing, dissatisfaction and the ability to bind ourselves to the outside world, to feel another atmosphere. Emotions also have to do with intuition, perception and sensibility.

Intellect

It is through the thinking that ideas and concepts can be absorbed, fantasized or articulated. The intellect is linked to the thinking, to the ideas and theory.

Volition

It is a wider concept than the will. We narrowed down the word will as to the idea of wanting something or not. Volition goes around that idea, but it is more than that. It has something to do with impulsivity, relevance and perseverance. The strong desire to something and the aggressiveness also relate with aspects of the soul.

Conscience

It is an inner voice that whispers, criticizing our actions and those of others, as well. The voice that accuses and complains sounds an alarm within us. It does not have the power of decision, but of judgment.

Free will

It is the core and the main axis of the soul. It is the greatest power of the soul; it is the ability to choose and decide.

Conscious

It is the surface of psychic life where consciousness can be found. It is the area where emotion, intellect and will appear. It is the field where thought, feeling and will interact with each other and it is also the place where are we can access all the data we have.

Unconscious

It is the result of traces received by inheritance added to the synthesis of our life experiences. All we have lived up to now is recorded within the unconscious."[1]

---

[1] Dr. Fabio Damasceno, OFFICE OF INNER HEALING, 1st Edition, AM Publisher IFC.

Even though we are so complex, there is nothing in the human being that cannot be repaired, corrected or transformed. The Bible teaches us that we must not conform to this world, but seek transformation through the renewing of our thoughts and mind. Despite great traumas that may still reside in the unconscious part of our minds, there is hope for us. God has an excellent restorer: the Holy Spirit. With our cooperation, He can cause us to remember situations that were once hidden in the back of our minds, bringing everything to the surface, which begins the healing, setting our soul free.

The first big step is to have a desire to change, the second step is to recognize that we need help, and the third step is to confess. From that point on, other things will be added, because the desire of each individual opens the door for God to act.

The will is the favor of all of mankind's decisions, but God does not interfere with it because He is just and He does not break His laws. The Lord does not interfere with free will; each individual has to decide. In Deuteronomy, chapter 28, it clearly reveals to us that mankind has the right to choose between good and evil, blessing or cursing. The Lord even gives us a tip on what we should choose:

"Now choose life, so that you and your children may live ..." (Deuteronomy 30:19).

Today, we can see the consequences of the wrong choices that many people have made. Some even end up dying because of drugs, adultery, promiscuity, sexual perversion and so many other things.

Learn to choose well, choose Christ. He is life. Give your future to Him and be aware that something very special will be reserved for you.

There was a queen in England who used to say that she feared men's prayers more than a fleet of warships that were trying to come against her nation. A prayer of intercession is one of the most powerful weapons that we have to bring destruction to the fortresses of hell. And in ways I was not aware of, God began to raise up prayer intercessors around me.

Despite the fact that I felt almost hopeless, in the bottom of my heart there was still a desire to obtain an answer to all my questions. Would it be possible for me to be completely set free in this area? I had already known ex-drug addicts, ex-robbers, ex-prostitutes, but I had never heard of anyone becoming an ex-homosexual.

However, at this point, I still was not serving the Lord, but I believed in His power to act in other people's lives. It was because I kept this faith that I witnessed a remarkable experience in the life of one particular family.

One day, I was at my beauty shop when a woman came in. She was absolutely terrified. Her name was Ana and she had just arrived from Porto Seguro with her family. She was running away from the police because she and her husband were cocaine addicts. They had found refuge in Ilhéus, but when her spouse was selling drugs in the city, the police showed up, and arrested him. Then, he was taken to a prison in Salvador. Obviously, this left Ana and her daughters in a very difficult situation.

After she told me her sad story, I looked closely into her

eyes. I told her I knew a lawyer; probably the only one who could resolve the matter. However, I was not in a position to talk about Him, because the life I was living at that time did not please Him. But I knew someone who could introduce her to Him. So I left all my clients at the beauty shop, and I took Ana to the house of Sister Noemi.

When we got there I said, "Sister Noemi, this lady is in need of a good lawyer; the One Who never loses. I brought her here so you can tell her about JESUS."

Then I turned back to Ana and said, "Tell her your problem. She will pray for you and everything will be solved."

Ana told her everything that had happened and Sister Noemi listened patiently. Then, with a look full of love, she said, "My daughter, open your heart to Jesus; surrender your life to Him, and know that He will send an angel to where your husband is. He will be reached and Jesus will resolve his matter."

Right then, on that very day, Ana made the decision to accept Jesus. Later, when she made her first visit to see her husband in Salvador, she had a huge surprise waiting for her. She arrived at the prison, but while they were taking her to where husband was supposed to be, she was told by one of the staff that her husband had been moved. He was now in the evangelical ward.

So she went to find him, still not understanding what had happened. She was actually afraid to tell him about her decision to serve Christ. When they saw each other again, they hugged and said simultaneously, "I have given my life to Jesus, and I received Him as my Savior."

It was a double miracle! Hallelujah!

The sentence of Ana's husband was reduced by many years. Today, he is a Pastor, and all his family serves Christ.

Even though God had used me to lead this woman toward the way of truth and I knew what He had done in her life, I still felt unable to give myself to Him. Sister Ana became a very fervent servant of God, and every time she saw me living the life I was living, she used to say, "Jorge Luís, I cannot believe it! You brought me to Jesus in your neighbor's house, but you continue to live a sinful life? One day God will set you free!"

As already mentioned, there are many factors that guide us to victory, and one of them is prayer. Even if you do not pray, if there is someone praying for you, then something will happen. Since my childhood, Sister Noemi used to take me to hear about Jesus. Later in life, my Aunts, Ana Célia, my father's sister, and Vera, my mother's sister, had converted to accept the Lord Jesus, also. Then they started praying for me. I did not know it, but God had already started to move both Heaven and Earth on my account.

I always had a very strong desire to win in life. This had been embedded within me because I had learned from my family that I needed to fight in order to win. I got in touch with my client's cousin who was living in the United States, and to my surprise, I received a post card with the picture of Central Park on it. Included with it was an invitation to spend a season in New York City to work with him.

I was excited about being able to make a change, but I was really excited about being able to earn U.S. dollars. I began to think and say that Brazil would now only be a place to visit for

the holidays. However, the Bible tells us that,
> "To humans belong the plans of the heart, but from the LORD comes the proper answer of the tongue" (Proverbs 16:1).

With an invitation in my hands, my dreams began to sprout. I thought to myself, "I will become a good, professional hairdresser, and I will not need to be accountable to my family anymore." Then, I hurriedly began to prepare for my trip. I shared what I was about to do with my family, clients and friends, and then I left in search of my U.S. Visa.

After I received my passport, to save time, I decided to personally go to the U.S. consulate in Rio de Janeiro to obtain my Visa. I knew that the bus trip between Ilhéus and Rio would take a full day, and I would need to be absent from work for a few days. So I left my beauty shop in the responsibility of my employees.

I arrived late at the bus station and unfortunately the bus had already left. So, I took a taxi and managed to reach the bus on the road to Itabuna. After a few minutes of travelling, a young lady invited me to sit on the seat across from her. She started talking about the reason for her trip—her father's death. He was the Pastor of a Baptist church for many years—and looking at me, she said, "When you entered the bus, God told me that He has a great plan for your life."

I asked her, "In my life?"

"Yes," she said. I will tell you a testimony that I heard in the church where I go in Rio de Janeiro. It is the story of a man who had his life completely transformed by Jesus. He was a transvestite, and he was sick with AIDS in a hospital at Barra da Tijuca. In that hospital, someone told him that Jesus could transform and heal his life. He believed and gave his life to God. Then God performed a great miracle and gave this man a new life, healing, freedom and total transformation. The Lord also gave him a wife and a son, who I met during his visit to my church.

She continued to say, "Write down my phone number on your notepad because one day you will call to tell me what God has done for you."

That girl did not know me, but God had shown her what was going on within me. Her spiritual eyes could see what was inside of me.

I thought she was very brave to talk about anything that relates to homosexuality because today it is a very controversial subject. But let's be realistic, despite society wanting to be liberal and believing they are doing so by legalizing homosexual marriages or approving laws that benefit homosexuals, we need to analyze this culture like any other cultural concept or theory in light of the Bible. Why? Because the Word of God "... is a lamp for my feet, a light on my path" (Psalm 119:105).

In Romans 1:25-27 it says,

> "They exchanged the truth about God for a lie, and worshiped and served created things rather than the Creator—who is forever praised. Amen. Because of this, God gave them over to shameful lusts. Even their women exchanged natural sexual relations for unnatural ones. In the same way the

men also abandoned natural relations with women and were inflamed with lust for one another. Men committed shameful acts with other men, and received in themselves the due penalty for their error."

- In 1 Corinthians 6:9-11, the Apostle Paul said, "Or do you not know that wrongdoers will not inherit the kingdom of God? Do not be deceived: Neither the sexually immoral nor idolaters nor adulterers nor men who have sex with men nor thieves nor the greedy nor drunkards nor slanderers nor swindlers will inherit the kingdom of God. And that is what some of you were. But you were washed, you were sanctified, you were justified in the name of the Lord Jesus Christ and by the Spirit of our God."

- God condemns the behavior of the homosexual and promises to judge not only those who practice it, but also the ones who consent to the practice. God loves all people, but because He is a "just" God, He must judge all sinful behavior. This doesn't mean that He takes pleasure in men's death—not even in the death of an unrighteous person. This is why He prepared a way out for the homosexual—JESUS.

We understand that some people in the church at Corinth had serious character issues, but when they met Jesus, they were cleansed, regenerated and transformed by God's power.

When we recognize that we need His help and run toward His open arms, then He brings the solution to our problems.

God has created mankind in His image and likeness. He created man and woman, but Satan wanted to disrupt this relationship by trying to hurt God's image. However, Christ was sent to heal, transform and set mankind free, that's why He is the solution to every problem, including homosexuality.

Even before Jesus began His ministry, He was asked to do something that resulted to a very important miracle that is vital to our lives today. On this occasion He did not revive the dead; neither did He heal the blind. But, as evidenced in John, chapter two, His first miracle was to transform water into wine. By performing this miracle, the Lord wanted to show us that only He can change the most difficult circumstances in our lives.

We have the free will to live our lives as we please; God has given us all the freedom to do that. But one day, we will be accountable to Him. Now, I have good news for you. If you wish to have your life changed, know that He can transform you into a new creature and everything will be new in your life.

It is written in 2 Corinthians 5:17,

"If anyone is in Christ, the new creation has come:
The old has gone, the new is here!"

I heard all that the girl told me on the bus, and I kept her phone number safe in my notepad. We then arrived at our final destination. She went on her own way, and I went to the American consulate to obtain my Visa.

Being able to receive my Visa and travel to the U.S. would

mean that my dream would be coming true. I was waiting anxiously for that. However, we may have many dreams, but it is God Who helps fulfill them in our lives.

After I arrived at the consulate's office, I entered the queue, filled out the application form and waited to be interviewed. During the interview, the Supervisor only asked me which city I intended to go to. I told him that I would be going to New York City. He then took my passport, gave me a ticket number and told me to come back in the afternoon to get my Visa. This was all I ever wanted. So, I left very happy, dreaming of my arrival in the U.S.

When I returned in the afternoon, I received my passport and my Visa. However, over the Visa stamp there was a word written in red: VOID. How frustrating it was! All my plans were undone and my hopes ended.

Today, I understand that it was the hand of God that interrupted my trip. The Word says, the door He closes, no man can open. He is sovereign over all things. John 13:7 tells us that many times we won't immediately understand what God is doing, but in the future, we certainly will.

However, at this point in my life, that didn't help me. I was so distressed with this news that I decided to spend some time in São Paulo. That is, until I could cool myself down and collect my thoughts. I phoned one of my clients' sisters, who always hosted me when I used to go there to take some of those specialized courses. So, that night, I decided to travel to São Paulo to seek comfort and peace.

When I arrived in São Paulo, my friend, Iraci, picked me up.

When she found out what had happened to me, she talked me into working in São Paulo. She told me there were great beauty salons there, and I could have an incredible career there. She said I could even earn as much money there as in the U.S.

Her daughter, Márcia, arranged an interview for me with the owner of the beauty salon, Jacques Janine. This was a famous international chain of beauty salons. After the interview, I did a trial shift, and I was later hired. Then, I asked my aunt, who lived in Aracajú, to spend some time in Ilhéus to help me look after my beauty shop.

The beginning in São Paulo was not easy. The life style was very different, and I had to adapt to this new world. I started to make more homosexual friends, and I began to attend bars and nightclubs. I remember on one occasion, I was in a very famous nightclub and amid all the noise, I told one of my colleagues, "Did you know that Jesus died on the cross for us and that He can transform our lives?"

Laughing, he said, "If Jesus could transform our lives, then what are you doing here? And, why hasn't He transformed you?"

I said, "I do not know, but I know He can."

I desired to know the transforming power of Christ in my life. During my childhood, all I ever heard about Jesus was that He could do miracles, and even though up to this point I had never experienced anything like that in my own life, I truly believed in His power. Even without having a true relationship with Him, I witnessed His manifestation in Ana's life. This was the same woman I had taken to the house of my sister, Noemi, so she could hear about the Lord. She received a miracle, and both she and her husband had their lives completely transformed and restored by God.

One morning, when I arrived home from a nightclub, I decided to watch the news on TV. When I turned it on, it was showing a Christian program. The music that was playing got my attention. Soon I realized there was a message which said, "SOS of LIFE; give us a call and receive a message of life." I wrote down the phone number that appeared on the TV, and as soon as I arrived at work, I called the number.

"Jesus loves you. How can I help you?" said a young lady from the other side of the line.

A bit shy, I asked her, "Can Jesus transform the life of a homosexual?"

She said, "Come again?"

So, I asked again, "Can Jesus transform the life of a homosexual?"

Then, she replied, "I do not know you, and what I am about to do now is not allowed, but my name is Aritânia, and I want to give you that answer personally. I want to do it today, because God has a great work to do in your life."

We agreed to meet later at the Sé metro station. Aritânia was waiting for me next to the ticket office. When I came close, she removed from her handbag two VHS tapes and gave them to me, saying, "The answer to your question is here. Listen carefully, because God will speak to you."

I was so curious to watch those tapes that once I got home, I didn't even take a shower. I went straight to the TV to watch them. To my surprise, it was the same testimony the lady on the bus had shared with me about a year before, during my trip from Ilhéus to Rio de Janeiro.

During this time, I was living with another man, and right when the message began, he started to make fun of me. I clearly realized that the devil was furious at me for listening to anything that had to do with this type of miracle, and he was using my partner to intimidate me. However, I continued to watch the tapes.

I cried so much after watching this testimony. I felt deeply touched by something supernatural. In that moment, I told God, "God, if you have done all of this in that man's life, then you can do it in mine, too."

When God designs a plan for us, He moves Heaven and Earth to fulfill it. When I have an opportunity to preach about the way God works, I say that when He wants to do something, He uses what is available to Him—whether it's the unrighteous, or a Japanese person who has never spoken Portuguese before, the circumstances, a dream, or a testimony. I know that in these first few chapters, He is already speaking to you; and He will continue to do so. You must only have a desire to listen.

I now had a desire to listen, but I was a slave to sin, and I had no strength to leave it. I knew I was wrong; my behavior did not do me any good, but I just did not know how to be free from sin. However, there is a solution for all who want to come out of any sinful lifestyle— JESUS—He is the truth that sets us free. Hallelujah! He truly sets people free.

At this moment, São Paulo did not impress me anymore. I

was not happy to remain there. Today, I understand that all my dissatisfaction was due to the sin I was living in. When we do not know true peace, we live in search of a temporary peace and satisfaction, whether it's in drugs, prostitution, or many other things. But true peace can only come from the Lord Jesus. He said it Himself,

> "Peace I leave with you; my peace I give you. I do not give to you as the world gives" (John 14:27).

So, it was then that I decided to live in Salvador, the homeland of carnival, where I could work in a beauty salon that was part of the same chain that I was working in, in São Paulo. I broke up with the other man, and I arranged my move to Salvador.

On the day of my departure to Salvador, as soon as I arrived at the airport of Guarulhos in São Paulo, Aritânia, the young lady from the SOS of LIFE, surprised me. She had come there to give me a letter. She told me that she would be praying for me, and one day, I would phone her to tell her about what God had done in my life. I read it, and I kept it safe for a very long time with my other documents. I knew this wasn't just any letter. This was a prophetic word that came from God to my heart.

Chapter 3

WHERE WILL I GO FROM YOUR SPIRIT?

"In a desert land he found him, in a barren and howling waste" (Deuteronomy 32:10).

Salvador is just one of thousands of cities in our country. However, it is the only city with the name that reveals the person of our Lord Jesus, Who alone can save mankind from sin, freeing us from eternal death.

When I lived in Ilhéus, I traveled to Salvador a few times to attend seminars in the field of cosmetics. I also got to know the clubs, bars, and places that were frequented by homosexuals.

When I arrived, I was greeted by a homosexual friend I had met in São Paulo during his vacation. I stayed at his apartment, but not for very long. It seemed that his "friend" was jealous of me.

I was already working in a new salon within the Jacques Janine network, and the manager, who was also involved in a relationship with another man, invited me to live with them. The plan was for me to help them share their household expenses. However, it didn't take me long to realize that he also wanted more of a relationship with me as well. I did not allow this.

I didn't think this kind of promiscuity was right. Similarly, I did not agree with my colleagues who prostituted themselves.

It wasn't that I thought that I was better than they were; after all, I was in the same lifestyle. It was just that I hadn't let the devil take me to that level of sexual depravity. I thought that God could bless a relationship between two men or two women who remained faithful. However, the Word of God commands in Leviticus 18:22,

> "Do not have sexual relations with a man as one does with a woman; that is detestable."

There are three kinds of love: Phileo, Eros and Agape. The first is the brotherly love, without any interest. The second is sexual love, which is released after the wedding as a gift from God to mankind. The latter is unconditional love, revealed to us through Jesus.

Because I had not agreed to get involved with my manager, he started to harass me at work. As I was new to the area, I had to make it a priority to meet new clientele, and unfortunately, he was the one who was responsible for referring clients to me. However, because he was upset that I wouldn't have anything to do with him sexually, he did not send a single person my way. I spent days without doing anyone's hair.

The difficulties increased, and the situation was unbearable. I contacted a friend who was opening a salon in Brasilia, the capitol city of Brazil. I had already decided to move there.

Days later, I came home one night to find my bags were packed and sitting by the door. Again, I was put out of the house. I did not know what to do because I did not know a lot of people in Salvador. Where would I go at this time of night? Then I remembered Barbara. She was a friend I had met in a homosexual environment. After calling her and explaining my situation to her, she told me to come and meet her. When I got there, she was with a friend, who was also a lesbian. They took me to a place in Itapuã.

When we arrived, the hostess told us to sleep outside because it was very hot inside the room—outside would be much cooler. Once I got outside and settled down, I realized I had been taken to sleep in a voodoo yard. I was a little scared at first, when I observed those images and candles, but even though I didn't have any fellowship with God, I was not afraid. I took my mattress, settled down and went to sleep.

When I woke up the next morning, I felt like I had won a major battle. Even though I had no money, I still didn't have to sleep on the streets or under a bridge. When I went to work that day, I shared what had happened to me the night before with a makeup artist who worked with me. He was touched by my situation and invited me to spend a few days with him, but only until things got better. I accepted the invitation, but just because I had nowhere else to go.

I was already unmotivated to stay at work because my manager had a real hatred for me. Today, I know that all things work together for the good of those who love God. He used this situation to take me to a better place, but at the time, I didn't have an awareness of such things. God has a plan for each person. He has a special plan for your life. He loves you, and

He sent His Son to die on the cross for you.

That day, after work, I went for a walk at the Iguatemi shopping mall, it is the largest one in São Paulo. Strolling around on the third floor, I saw that there was a very busy salon. I decided to stop and observe it for a while. After a few minutes, one of the employees came out and walked over to me. I asked her, "Do you have any positions available for a hairdresser?"

Very politely, she said, "A position has just opened up." She then suggested that I speak with the receptionist to set up an interview appointment with the owner of the salon.

I walked over to the receptionist, but was informed that the owner was out of town. He was supposed to return soon. I thanked her for her attention and left. That's when I remembered that before I left São Paulo, one of my co-workers had told me about a popular hair salon in Salvador. I was told if I needed any help, I could look them up. As soon as I found his address, I contacted him and told him about the difficulties I was facing. He immediately took me to another franchise of that salon and made an appointment with the owner.

At the appointment, I told the owner I had worked in the Jacques Janine Salon of São Paulo, and now I was working for the same company in Salvador. The owner liked the references and asked me what my name was.

"Jorge Luís," I answered.

She then called one of the managers and said, "Neilda, show our new employee which chair is his."

On the monitor, where she saw what was happening on the salon floor, she showed me the last chair. Hallelujah! The Word of God declares that the last shall be first. Amen!

The next day, I packed my work supplies, which I always kept with me, and went straight to my new job. The salon was extremely busy. There were 25 hairdressers in all. Everyone earned a very good salary of around $2,500 a month, which didn't include the tips. I vigorously started to work. It was not hard to establish my new clientele—I was a professional, and I was good. I had come from São Paulo, and the clients liked my work.

Later, for one week, I went to an International Congress convention in Buenos Aires, Argentina. When I returned, a former hairdresser wanted to take my chair. He claimed to be a close friend of the owner of the salon and had already put his stuff on my bench. The other colleagues who worked there had faced problems with him, so they made a request for me to stay. Today, I know that they were used by God to keep me there, because something important was about to happen.

Just as the Lord's angels encamp around those who fear God and protect them, the devil walks into our surroundings, roaring like a lion, seeking whom he may devour. From the time I was in my mother's womb, when she decided to give me up for adoption, there was a war being fought over my life, and it intensified every day.

The enemy did not want me to stay there. Even though there were fifteen homosexuals among the staff, there were also two servants of God: Fatima and Zaíra. In addition, many people were already praying for me—my aunts, the lady I met on the bus to Rio de Janeiro, Aritânia and many others. The spiritual atmosphere was already shifting in favor of my salvation. God has a time and a specific place to carry out His plan, and He works in favor of those who hope in Him. Although I did not know it yet, He was beginning to prepare many surprises for me.

Sister Zaíra, my co-worker at the salon, was a very kind and friendly young lady. She always tried to serve me when I needed help. In general, the others were selfish and greedy, but since she was a Christian, she was different. One day, we went to have coffee and started to talk. At first, we spoke about hair color and haircuts, but soon we began to talk about the main subject—JESUS. She said she had been watching me since the first day I walked into that room, and she knew God would do a great work in my life. I found it a little funny. I thought to myself, "Am I really hearing this word again?"

I lived in Ilhéus, Aracaju, Uruçuca, and João Pessoa. I went through Rio de Janeiro. I moved to São Paulo, and finally, I came to Salvador. Wherever I went, there was always someone, who even without knowing me, talked about the great work that God would do in my life. There is no getting away from the Lord! He had surrounded me in every way and was already about to rescue me; it only depended upon me to make the right decision.

Even though I had heard of Jesus since my childhood and believed in the transforming power of God, I was too disappointed with the Church. During my teenage years, at the church I was attending, there was a scandal that involved a pastor and a homosexual man. Later on, there was another incident that involved two young lesbians. I don't need to mention again the sexual abuse I suffered from a seminary student, who went on to become a pastor.

The devil used these facts and managed to extinguish any possibility that I might ever step into a church again, let alone be a part of one. Even though I was living a life of sin, I never stopped believing that God is powerful and that Jesus died for me on the cross. He has risen, and He is alive.

During our conversation, Zaíra talked about a sister who could help me. But after dealing with so many frustrations with other believers and the church, I only listened to be polite. I knew I was not interested in her invitation.

My life was very different. I had a good salary in the salon where I was working. I moved into a new apartment. I began spending time at nightclubs, bars, and at the beach. I wasn't missing my friends. I started to wear designer clothing, French perfumes, and I even had a cell phone, which was considered to be a real luxury at the time.

However, even though it appeared that I had it all together, there was still a very big void in my heart. I tried to fill it with holiday activities, clothes, travel, friends, and moving from city to city—I tried to seek joy and satisfaction, but I did not know that this feeling could only be found in the person of Jesus Christ.

And God went on around me. One day, when we were extremely busy at the salon, I was given a new client who wanted to have her hair done, but just by me. We were talking about what she wanted me to do, when she interrupted me. She looked into my eyes and said, "God told me to come here to tell you something. He has a great work to accomplish in your life."

"Again," I thought.

She then continued, "He also asked me to tell you about something that happened in my life before I came to know Jesus. My family doesn't even know about this. You see, I was in a homosexual relationship for many years. To the natural eye, I didn't see how to free myself from that relationship, but when I met Jesus, I was freed from the feeling that bound me. And God wants to do the same in your life."

Before she left the salon, she gave me a brochure and invited me to visit an evangelical church. We became friends, and we talked whenever she came to the salon. I even visited the church, but I still did not make any decision to accept Jesus.

There were many people praying for me, asking God to touch my life and draw me closer to Him, so I could have a real experience with Him. Among them was one of my aunts. She was a part of a group who did deliverance at an evangelical church, and she never ceased to pray for our family. When she heard that one of my brothers was involved with drugs and about the lifestyle I was living, she decided to stay at home and fast and pray for our deliverance. That week, she would not go out to pray for others; she would stay home and pray for us. She began to pray on Sunday morning and that same evening, my brother went to the Assemblies of God church that was close to where he lived. He gave his life to the Lord Jesus. Since then, by God's mercy, he has remained strong in Him.

◂Prayer and fasting are powerful weapons to destroy

strongholds. Even if it takes a long time to see your prayers answered—persevere—because they have been heard by the Father, and He will give you the victory.

Just as it happened to Daniel,

"Since the first day that you set your mind to gain understanding and to humble yourself before your God, your words were heard, and I have come in response to them" (Daniel 10:12).

Even if the enemy tries to rob you of your blessing, the Lord will send angels to fight for you.

I had already adapted very well in Salvador. I had a busy life. I got to work at nine in the morning and only went home after I had taken care of all my customers. I knew the nightclubs, beaches, gay bars, and I was engaged in a homosexual relationship. Outwardly, everything seemed to be fine. I believed to be happy and loved, but it was pure deception.

In fact, there is no love in this type of relationship. What exists is only passion and lust, as we read in Paul's letter to the Romans,

"For this reason God gave them up to vile passions. For even their women exchanged the natural use for what is against nature. Likewise also the men, leaving the natural use of the woman, burned in their lust for one another, men with men committing what is shameful, and receiving in themselves the penalty of their error which was due" (Romans 1:26, 27, NKJV).

True love is very different than this blind, insane lust that leads to physical and spiritual death. The existence of happiness and true love between homosexual couples is just the devil's lies. Behind all of this, there is a lot of frustration, for God can never bless a relationship that is completely contrary to the principles of His holiness.

Even homosexual intercourse is incompatible with the anatomy and functioning of the human body. Sodomy is contrary to nature and to God's plan. Therefore, it has serious both natural and spiritual consequences. There is a high rate of cancer that appears in both men and women that comes from this sexual act. We also know that there is an evil spirit that works specifically in this area, which causes many lives to suffer and even die from this practice.

But those who do not repent of their deeds, Paul exhorts,

"Do not be deceived: neither the sexually immoral nor idolaters nor adulterers nor men who have sex with men nor thieves nor the greedy nor drunkards nor slanderers nor swindlers will inherit the kingdom of God" (1 Corinthians 6:9, 10).

At that time, I did not know anything about it. Although I had already heard some things, I could not discern these truths. But thanks be to God, Who saved me from spiritual blindness!

Chapter 4

SEARCHING FOR HELP

> "Call to me and I will answer you and tell you great and unsearchable things you do not know"
> (Jeremiah 33:3).

One day, I left the apartment/hotel where I lived with one decision in my heart: I would give my life to Jesus. Once I got to work, I called Zaíra and said, "Take me to any believer's home because I want to give my life to Jesus. If He can change me, I will surrender my life to Him."

She didn't know whether to laugh or cry. That was all she wanted to hear from me. She had been praying for a long time that God would touch my heart.

"Are you kidding me?" she asked.

"I've never been so serious," I replied.

Quickly, Zaíra went to the reception desk and asked them not to send any customers to us during lunchtime that day. She told the receptionist we were going to meet another client from the mall.

All morning long, hour after hour, she approached me and asked, "Are you really going? No kidding, right?"

My homosexual colleagues began to mock me. All they

wanted to do was to try and bring me down. They obviously didn't want me to go Zaíra's friend's house. However, I was determined; I stayed firm to my decision.

At midday, she took me by the arm and we left. As soon as we arrived, I was invited to sit on the sofa and wait. Truthfully, I wasn't prepared for what was about to happen. I thought that I would be meeting with an old lady. Maybe she would be fat, with white hair, and she would definitely be wearing a long skirt. However, to my surprise, I was greeted by a beautiful young lady. When she came into the room she was smiling, and she had very black hair.

I was a little embarrassed because she came right up to me and hugged me. Then she saluted me with a peaceful gesture. She told me that she had already been praying for me since Zaíra had told her about me. She knew that one day God would bring me there. Then she called me to go into her office with her. She closed the door and asked me to sit on the couch. Then she said, "Feel free to say whatever you want, because anything you say will only be between us and the Holy Spirit of God."

A little shy and with great difficulty, I began to open up my heart and told her a little about my story. I spoke of the rejection at birth, the frustrations with my adoptive father, the sexual abuse I had suffered, and the life I was living in homosexuality. At one point, I looked into her eyes and noticed that it was like she was laughing. I was embarrassed, and I wanted to leave immediately. I thought to myself, "Here I am, pouring out something that is so sad in my life, and here she is, a person who does not even know me well, and she wants to laugh at me?"

Then she looked at me and said, "Do you know why I'm laughing? It is because God is showing me the lovely work that He will accomplish in your life."

Now, I could not hold back the tears. "How could this be happening?" I asked myself. She spoke as if she had read my mind! Today, I know it was the Holy Spirit of God Who revealed to her what was going on in my mind.

I felt something very strong inside of me, and still crying I asked her, "Can God really get rid of this life I'm living? He can change my way, my feelings and my emotions?"

"God will change you completely, my son," she said to me. She was completely confident that she was telling me the truth.

"And what should I do for Him to change me?" I asked.

"Give your life to Jesus. Make a covenant with Him, and from today, God will begin to work in your life."

I didn't even wait a moment. I stood to my feet and repeated this prayer, "Lord Jesus, I open my heart and I invite you to enter it. Forgive me of my sins; wash me with Your blood and write my name in Your book of life."

When I finished the prayer, she told me to repeat another prayer to renounce all the sinful practices and any alliance I might have had with the kingdom of darkness. Then she raised her hands and said she would pray for me. I felt my body become light, and when I went to say "amen," I could not; it was like my tongue was curled. I was a little confused, not knowing what was happening to me at that time. I began to think that the devil was using my body.

But then she said, "You can't talk because you were baptized in the Holy Spirit."

It may seem that it came too early, but the Bible says that he who confesses and forsakes sin, receives mercy. God had immediately filled me with His Spirit; the struggle that was to come is almost beyond words.

Before ending our session, she advised me to give up the relationship, clothes, gifts and all that was connected to the homosexual world and lifestyle. Holding my phone, she said a prayer to block any and all calls that could hinder my walk with Christ. She then warned me, "Still today, I want us to pray together, because we need to start a campaign of fasting and prayer for your release."

She hugged me and said, "The peace of the Lord, my brother!"

I left that room feeling weightless! As I was leaving her house, her husband, who had not heard anything of our conversation, called me to come into the room where he was. He was watching a videotape of the International Convention ADHONEP, in Rio de Janeiro, which was being led by an American pastor, Benny Hinn. (ADHONEP is an international Association of Christian businessmen and women who seek to share the Good News of the Gospel.)

The video had a testimony of a young man who had been infected with the HIV virus, but was cured after a prayer. When I finished watching that part, he insisted that I watch it again. Politely, I accepted. I watched it three times, so it was etched into my memory. I thanked him and went back to work with

Zaíra.

I left willing to face everything and everyone to achieve the promise that God had made me that day. It didn't matter whether it included losses or gains; I wanted to be free.

> "Then Jesus said to His disciples, 'If anyone desires to come after Me, let him deny himself, and take up his cross, and follow Me. For whoever desires to save his life will lose it, but whoever loses his life for My sake will find it'" (Matthew 16:24, 25, NKJV).

When I got back to work, was there excitement! My colleagues laughed and made fun of me. All of them began to criticize me for my decision to walk with Jesus, but I did not care what they said. I wanted to achieve the victory that Jesus had promised me.

Later, in the apartment/hotel where I lived, I took all the clothes, photos, souvenirs and everything else that involved the homosexual world and destroyed it. I remembered I had a Bible that I had stored away for many years. So I got it out. I knelt down and began to pray, confirming my covenant with Jesus. I knew the Bible was the Word of God, so I asked Him to speak to me through it. When I opened the Scriptures, I came across a passage from Ezekiel 33:26,

> "You rely on your sword, you do detestable things, and each of you defiles his neighbor's wife. Should you then possess the land?"

This was the first word I received from God to return to Him, promising me new life, new direction and a release to my soul.

When God sees a true desire in someone to turn from their sin, He takes care of the rest,

> "For since the beginning of the world men have not heard nor perceived by the ear, nor has the eye seen any God besides You, who acts for the one who waits for Him" (Isaiah 64:4).

It's not enough to say that we want to; it must be proved with an attitude or desire to change our lives. Repentance involves a change of attitude and direction. It generates a new beginning, a new way of living—new habits, thoughts, friendships and a new way of doing things.

> "Therefore, if anyone is in Christ, the new creation has come: the old has gone, the new is here!" (2 Corinthians 5:17).

Since I broke up with the young man I was in relationship with, I began to change my life. I knew there were two Christian guys, who needed help with the cost of their apartment, so I decided to live with them. I gave up the apartment/hotel comfort to live in a single room, with those brothers.

I also changed my daily routine. I fasted every morning, worked most of the day listening to gospel music on a walkman, read the Bible at home before going to bed, and many times woke up during the night to pray. Even if I spent the night awake praying, I could still work normally the next day because my strength was renewed.

Many mornings I saw the daybreak. It wasn't because I had insomnia, but I was seeking God unceasingly. At those moments, God would speak to me a lot, and that is where He healed my soul. He brought to light so many facts that were forgotten—buried down inside of me—areas that needed healing. I remember one night, I asked God about the lack of a father and He showed me that He had always been my Father. He showed me His care in difficult moments of my life, and the deliverance He gave me even before I knew Him. Even if my biological or adoptive father had accepted me, they could have never met my needs like God, my Father did.

I started to have trouble at work because of the Name of Jesus. Everyone criticized me. They even wrote absurd things on the mirror about me, just trying to embarrass me in front of my customers. And to make things worse, that colleague who wanted to take my place when I went to Argentina, ended up working in the same room I was in. He was a spiritist, one more person to rise up against me. None of this mattered to me because greater is He that is in you, than he that is in the world!

None of this made me back off, either, because I was constantly praying and fasting. In addition, there was a group of sisters who helped me in prayer, week after week.

One morning, while walking down the hall, I knew that my boss wanted to talk to me. I went up to her office and she asked me what was going on. She asked, "Do you need therapy or some kind of help?" My colleagues had told her I was going crazy. She really liked me, and she wanted to help. She even asked if I wanted to be transferred to another salon, to smooth out everything I was going through. But God had something to do in that salon, and I could not overstep His timing. I didn't know what it was yet, but He always used some brothers to tell me and confirm that He still had a great work to do there.

With boldness, I told her that I would not be moved out of there until God told me it was time to go. Then I explained the reason for the trouble, "My colleagues do not accept the change in my life since I came here living a life like them, but now I have accepted Jesus as my Savior and He is freeing me of the life I led. However, my fight is not against them, but against the principalities and powers of darkness who work in their lives."

She had difficulty understanding me, since the natural man cannot receive the things of the Spirit of God: "... for they are foolishness unto him" (1 Corinthians 2:14).

When I came back to the salon, I realized that everyone expected me to be transferred, but I wasn't. There is a time determined by God for all things, and He gave me the victory to continue to stay there. It just wasn't the right time to leave.

The fight and the persecutions may come, but when the Lord gets up from His throne on our behalf, the demons fall away, our opponents are ashamed and confounded, and we see their defeat.

The Bible says that a man reaps what he sows. I say that God forgives our sin, but sin has its price, and we will reap the consequences. However, the Lord sustains us, because it is the

LORD'S mercies that we are not consumed, because His ==love never fails.==

Everything was going fine, and with Christ, I continued winning the battles, day after day. The fights I faced with coworkers were insignificant to me. I really had made a serious decision to stay close to Jesus. I changed my conversations and what I did in my leisure time, and my colleagues began to respect me as a Christian.

But one day, I was sitting in my chair, waiting for a customer, when my cell phone rang. The call was from the guy with whom I had been in relationship with. After I answered, he asked me, "So, is it true that now you are Christian?"

"Yes," I replied.

"There is no way we can get back together?" he asked.

"No, I'm living a life for Jesus," I said.

Then he asked, "Are you sitting down? I just want to say that I hope you do not have any symptoms of pneumonia, diarrhea, tuberculosis ..." And then he hung up.

I can't tell you explicitly all that he said on the phone, but he was pretty direct about him defiling me with the HIV virus. He clearly warned me about all the other diseases that resulted from it.

Satan will use whatever he can to scare servants of God. As the man saw that there was no chance of getting back together with me, he threatened me and wanted to scare me with the news of a disease.

After that call, I remembered what I had heard on the bus, years before, about the guy who was cured of HIV. I also remembered the tape I had watched of the testimony of someone being delivered from HIV on the day I gave my life to the Lord.

Although I didn't want to believe that man's threat, I remembered the times when he wanted to have sex without any protection. I did not understand why, especially when we lived in São Paulo, where the rate of HIV victims was very high. He must have already had it in his heart to infect me, but I was blind and could not see it. Sin blinds us; it blinds human knowledge.

The Word tells us the devil comes to steal, kill and destroy. That's what he wanted to do with me from the time I was in my mother's womb. That guy was not my real enemy; he was just another tool Satan was using to destroy my life. My fight was not against flesh and blood, but against principalities and powers, as it is written in Ephesians 6:12,

> "For our struggle is not against flesh and blood, but against the rulers, against the authorities, against the powers of this dark world and against the spiritual forces of evil in the heavenly realms."

Despite all of this, I could not believe that I was infected. I really thought it was just another threat to try and stop my walk with Christ. I continued my life, praying, fasting and living free from sin. Satan tempted me very often to get me to return to sin by bringing up memories and putting people in my path to proposition me, even at work.

I remember a client, a famous doctor in Salvador, who always treated me well. He had never made any attempt to solicit my attention. However, one day he asked me out. Gently,

I answered that I had become a servant of God and would not accept that kind of invitation. Then he told me he had always watched me and admired me.

He also told me he was a homosexual, and his boyfriend had died of HIV a few months before. He had provided the necessary assistance until his death, staying with him until the last moments of his life. Thank God, my decision to accept Jesus as my Savior was noticeable. I understood that from that day on, I should give up everything that connected me to the homosexual world.

This gave me the strength to reject the devil's trap. Fleeing from sin is the secret to obtaining victory in the Christian life.

> "Submit yourselves, then, to God. Resist the devil,
> and he will flee from you" (James 4:7).

According to psychology, man must not hold back his impulses because this creates frustration. But this theory does not consider the consequences of satisfying all of our fleshly desires. Everything is permissible, but not everything is beneficial. The day shall come when we will make account to God of everything we do with our bodies,

> "Do you not know that your bodies are temples
> of the Holy Spirit, who is in you, whom you have
> received from God? You are not your own; ..."
> (1 Corinthians 6:19).

To sin is to miss the mark God has destined for us. But from a scientific point of view, this concept is merely religious. It does not exist in the scientific community. Therefore, psychology does not consider the existence of sin, and consequently, the possibility of Divine deliverance for those who are bound by it. But I thank God for sending Jesus to help us straighten out our tortuous paths, so we can achieve all that He has planned for us.

Today, science has admitted that forgiveness brings healing to the body and soul. Psychologists say that forgiveness is good. I hope that, one day, they will also accept the existence of sin and its consequences. Thank God for all Christian psychologists who are light in an area that is still full of darkness.

One day, when I got to the work, a colleague invited me for coffee. I accepted his invitation, and we began to talk. He said, "Jorge, you're so young, smart, and beautiful. You have had so little time here in the salon, and you already earn the same living as the oldest person here. But I'll tell you something, this thing that these two crazy believers (he was referring to the two Christian sisters who worked with us), are trying to put into your head is a lie. You are hopeless; it will never change. You were born that way, and you will die like that."

This guy was involved with mysticism, and I could see that he was not the one who was really speaking. Instead, it was the enemy of our soul, the devil. However, I remembered the first word that God gave me when I accepted Jesus as my Savior,

"I will give you a new heart and put a new spirit in you; I will remove from you your heart of stone and give you a heart of flesh" (Ezekiel 36:26).

Immediately, I answered him, "God told me that He will transform my heart and my life. Although I don't feel it today, I know He will set me free."

After I said that he got angry and left grumbling. When Jesus was tempted by Satan in the desert, He overcame temptation through speaking the Word. (Matthew 4). God had given me a word of victory at the beginning of my walk with Christ, and I clung to it, believing that He would deliver me.

But our enemy does not give up so easily. When that colleague left, a war like I had never experienced unlocked in my mind. I heard voices that kept repeating, "Give it up, you will not be free." They persisted with such intensity that I got to the point where I couldn't work any more that day. I canceled the appointment with my clients, and I went home.

I had heard about spiritual warfare, but I had not faced anything like this. We know that the mind controls the whole body and when it gets out of balance, the whole body collapses. So the opponent's target is to reach the human mind, and thus, achieve disruption and confusion.

I was so confused I do not know how I got home. I believe that God sent angels to help me. As soon as I entered, I went to my room and began to pray. Crying out I said, "Lord, you promised to give me a new heart, but these voices tell me to give up!"

I kept praying and talking to God about His promise to free me. At that time, what kept coming to my mind were words of discouragement, frustration and scenes of all that I had practiced, while I was living in sin. After praying and crying a lot, I fell into a deep sleep.

During church services, I had heard people talk about dreams, visions or revelations, which they had seen, but I had not experienced anything like that. I prayed during the night, and I believed that God was listening to me, but nothing supernatural happened to me.

But while I slept that night, I had an interesting dream. I found myself in a big place like a shed, and with me was a young woman, who was about my height. She had curly hair that went down to her shoulders. She was wearing a dress that went down below her knees. I could not see her face because she was focused on a very bright light. In the dream, I heard a very loud voice repeatedly say, "This is the love I have for you."

When I woke up, it was a new day. I realized that the voices that told me to give up had gone away, and the bad memories had also ceased. Once I got to work, I called Zaíra to tell her everything that had happened to me. I asked her to explain to me what all of it meant because I still could not understand. When I started to tell her about the great spiritual battle that I had faced and the dream I had experienced, my phone rang. I stopped to answer the call. On the other end I heard a woman's voice greet me.

"Peace of the Lord, my son! You do not know me, but I am Sister Eduarda. My voice sounds like I'm a child, but I'm sixty-five years old. During the service in Pituba Church, I took your name to pray for you. Yesterday, while I was praying around 2:00 a.m., God gave me a vision. I saw you next to a young woman, who wore a dress just below the knees and had curly hair down to her shoulders. I could not see her face because she had a very strong light on it."

I was very impressed with that phone call because a person on the other side of town, almost unknown to me, called to testify about the same dream! But the Bible tells us that the testimony of two is true.

After I hung up from that call, I called Zaíra again. I said, "Zaíra, you will not believe what has just happened. Another sister, named Eduarda, called me up to tell me about a vision she had about me. However, the most interesting thing is that yesterday I had the same vision. I was asleep and I dreamt of a young woman who approached me. I saw her clothes and hair, but I did not see her face because there was a very strong light on it. During the dream, I heard a voice saying, 'This is the love I have for you.'"

Smiling, Zaíra said, "Jorge, do you know what this is? God is preparing a "Rebekah" for you!"

Chapter 5

FIREPROOF

"... the God who gives life to the dead and calls into being things that were not" (Romans 4:17).

The one thing that is good about a great battle is that when you win, you have a greater victory. While I was fighting that battle in my mind, I thought I would not win. However, when I resisted, comfort came to me.

"... weeping may stay for the night, but rejoicing comes in the morning" (Psalms 30:5).

The biggest difficulty for a homosexual is to be attracted to the opposite sex. But for God, nothing is impossible. As I already said, when we desire something and we work hard to obtain this from God, then God Himself takes over and works in our favor.

My decision for Christ was genuine, and I was willing to do anything. I wanted my freedom at any cost. It did not matter to me how many years I had lived as a homosexual because I had a promise from God for my life and this was what I relied upon. When I prayed, I asked God, "Change my life, Lord!"

I did not seek Christ because I was going through financial difficulties or because I was living in hunger or because I did not have anywhere to live. I sought Him because I wanted my freedom, and I wanted to change my life. This is why I was willing to pay any price to obtain my victory.

After I had that dream, something different started to happen. I began to have feelings in my heart that I thought were impossible—love for a woman. It was very different from the passion that I had before. I started to make plans and to dream about that young lady. My desire to meet her grew every day, and I started loving her even before I saw her. The true miracle was happening—God was beginning to transform water into wine!

Some time went by, and one day I accepted an invitation from a couple of friends of mine who were from an evangelical community to spend New Year's Eve in prayer with them. This was new for me! Now, the old friends had gone away and going out to nightclubs would not give me pleasure anymore. What would really give me joy was to seek God.

The month of December is always very busy for beauty salons, and on the day of the meeting with my friends, I got home from work very tired. I was in the shower, getting ready to go out, when I heard a very strong voice in my heart say, "Today, you will meet her!" The vision that I had seen of that young woman in my dream played over in my mind, and I was sure that I would meet her that night.

When I arrived at the meeting, I started to observe the people who were there. I was looking for her, but since I did not see her face in the dream, I did not know what she would look like. The service was a big blessing, and I could see the difference between celebrating New Year's Eve in the presence of Jesus and the way I used to do it. After the service, a young man named Samuel introduced me to some people and among them was the woman from my dream. I felt a bit frightened because it was the moment I had been waiting for. The light that covered her head made way to her face and promptly I shook her hand. My heart began to beat very fast.

After I was introduced to her, I went away and leaned against the wall. Then the scene in my dream repeated—she came toward me and we started to chat.

She asked me, "Where do you work?"

I replied, "At the Iguatemi shopping mall."

She continued, "What do you do?"

I said, "I am a hairdresser."

Then she said, "Ah! I am an aesthetician and makeup artist."

The most interesting thing is that I had even thought about the possibility of the woman in my dream being a hairdresser or aesthetician. In this, we could have a beauty salon together when we got married. It also caught my attention that she was wearing a bracelet that was identical to mine. It was a piece of jewelry that was very different from the ones found in the marketplace. It was made of many types of gold and there was a pendant of David's star. I never really liked wearing jewelry before I gave my life to Jesus, but days before, one of my clients who worked in a jewelry shop, insisted that I should buy one. It appeared that everything was being confirmed.

The final confirmation, that she was really the woman in my dream, was when one sister came toward her and made a comment about her hair. I understood that her hair was longer and that she had just had a haircut that day. God had shown me in my dream, a woman with short hair, around the shoulders. Then, I was certain that God had prepared each detail of our meeting.

As soon as we said our goodbyes, there was already a very strong feeling in my heart—one of pure and true love. If I already loved her before I even met her, then you can only imagine how I felt afterward. I could not stop thinking about her. It was difficult to fall asleep after everything that had happened.

When I returned to work the following morning, it was a bank holiday. To my surprise, she came to the beauty salon so we could talk. We left together to have a cup of coffee and as soon as we sat down she told me how interesting our meeting was. She said that before she met me she knew she would find me. Then, we talked for a very long time, until she said, "Let's start from the beginning; we will pray and fast for fifteen days and then see what the Lord wants."

I was so anxious to start a relationship with her that fifteen days seemed too long; but because I wanted to obey God, I accepted. Every day that went by, my love for her grew.

God is amazing! He calls into being things that were not. He generated in my heart a feeling that I had not ever experienced before. From that time, the love for a woman became a part of me. God started doing the biggest of all miracles a man can receive—the miracle of transformation! Nothing can be compared to that, and it is priceless, the transformation that only Jesus can do. Only He can transform water into wine within us.

All potters know that the clay needs to go through many stages until it is transformed into a vase. With me, it wouldn't be any different! I was at the hands of the Potter, being prepared every day. I was leaving behind and getting rid of the pride, arrogance, vanity, selfishness and many other feelings in my life that needed to be removed. I was also being shaped through all the humiliation I went through at the beauty salon that I used to work at, but many times, still being mistreated at the hands of people who called themselves brothers, too.

However, it was all part of the process. After being shaped, the potter takes the vase to the fire so it can be refined; only then, will it be ready for use. If the vase can withstand the fire, it is ready to fulfill its purpose; but if it cracks, it will break, and then it will go through the whole process again. God is the perfect Potter! (Jeremiah 18).

Despite all the battles I was going through, everything was fine. After all, I wasn't part of the kingdom of dark shadows anymore. I was not pleasing the devil any longer; therefore, it was natural that he would come against me. It was then that I realized that my body wasn't well; I had some pains and was feeling ill.

One day, I was in horrible pain. I thought it was my kidneys; I couldn't stand properly, so I decided to go home. I was at the door when I remembered that I had forgotten an important hairbrush at my workstation. Since my colleagues always tried to irritate me by hiding or stealing my stuff, I went back to get it. As I was putting my hairbrush in my drawer, a young man of around twenty-eight years old grabbed my arm and said, "Can you finish cutting my hair, please?"

I saw that his hair was done only on one side, but I still thought that his request was a bit strange. How would I finish cutting the hair of someone who had started with another colleague? However, even in my pain, I had to comply with the manager's order.

As soon as I finished the job, he looked at his hair and said, "I really like the haircut! You just won a client and a friend." Then, he removed a business card from his pocket and gave it to me, saying, "My name is Alex. I am a doctor who specializes in infectious diseases, and I work in a few hospitals here in Salvador."

At this moment, once again, a few images came to my mind. It was like a film—the testimony I had heard on the bus, the tape that Aritânia had given me in São Paulo, the video recording of the healing testimony in the ADHONEP Conference, and finally, the threat that the man made to me over the phone.

On the other hand, I could see the care God had taken with my life. As the Bible says, He was working for my good. Since the time I left to go to Rio de Janeiro until my decision for Christ, the Lord was preparing me for this moment. However, I thought that it was only a coincidence. This could happen to others, but not to me.

I kept the doctor's business card safe because I was shockingly seeing the symptoms of AIDS starting to appear. Dr. Alex became my client, friend and doctor, because he used to come to the beauty salon almost weekly, and he was the one who prescribed that I take the HIV test. At this stage, I was ready for anything that would come before me. My first complication came in the form of a kidney infection, which was the cause of my back pains.

On one specific occasion, Dr. Alex told me that what he really feared was I had Kaposi's sarcoma. This is a type of cancer that is very common in patients who are HIV positive. In these cases, the treatment for the patients is chemotherapy or radiation, which generally weakens the defense mechanism of the body; it can also cause one to die quickly.

However, the reason I received Jesus in my life was not to get anything material from Him. I surrendered to Him so He could transform my life and my lifestyle. I was in His hands, and I wanted my freedom.

When I told Zaíra about my illness she was shocked. She said, "Jorge, no! There must be something wrong, because now you are a servant of God."

I said, "Zaíra, I couldn't die without Jesus in my life; otherwise, I would go to hell. But now, I am in His hands."

So I continued living my life, keeping my routine of prayer, fasting and reading the Bible. One evening, after a very tiring day, when I got home I could do nothing, but pray. While I was praying my cell phone rang. It was one sister who wanted to pray with me. She did not know anything about my health condition, but right at the beginning of the prayer she began to pray in spiritual tongues and she prophesied. God began to speak to me through this sister, but for no reason, the call got cut off.

Instantly, I phoned her back, and she told me, "Brother, the call got cut off, but I know what God wants to tell you this evening. He tells you, 'Behold I send you angels in your favor, My beloved servant, because great is the storm that will come upon you. But do not fear, for I am with you.'"

It was already nighttime. The next day I only worked until 2:00 p.m., and then I went to a service at a sister's house. I slept the rest of the night. When I woke up that next morning, I got up and began to get ready for work. While taking a shower, I felt my lower body burning. It was the Kaposi's sarcoma. My heart went cold! I was overtaken with a mixture of fear, anguish, sadness and despair. Then, I wrapped myself in a towel and went to my bedroom.

I prayed, "God, I am in Your hands!" It was the only words I could say at that moment.

I decided not to go to work that day. I phoned the beauty salon and told my manager that I would not be coming in. I stayed at home, writing about everything that God had done in my life since I had surrendered my life to Him. I only left to go to the service.

Every Wednesday, as always, I fasted in the morning and then gathered with some sisters who were helping me by praying for my freedom. The service used to take place in the afternoon on the balcony of a house. When I arrived there that day, I kneeled down and started to praise God. Meanwhile, they were singing a song that said, "Jesus saves; He saves."

As soon as I began to worship, I felt the presence of God in that place, and the sister who was leading the worship started to lead out in prayer. Soon after, she changed the lyrics of the song to "Jesus heals; He heals!" At this moment, she came close to me. I still had my eyes closed. Then I felt her hand upon my head. A very powerful anointing came upon my body while we all praised the Lord in spiritual tongues.

When the service finished, the sister told me, "God has healed you today!" She did not know about my illness. I believed that God had used her to minister healing to me. Then, I went quickly to the bathroom to confirm the miracle I believed I had received. However, the cancer was still there. I began to fear again, but I heard a voice, like the roar of rushing waters, tell me, "Great is the storm, but do not fear, for I am with you!"

It came to my heart, the desire to go to work after that service, but as I was leaving, a lady stopped me and said, "Brother, before you go, please read Psalm 103, because God has a word for you there.

I left the house, and as I walked I read the Psalm, which said,

> "Praise the Lord, my soul; all my inmost being, praise his holy name. Praise the Lord, my soul, and forget not all his benefits—who forgives all your sins and heals all your diseases ..."
> (Psalm 103:1-3).

I arrived at the beauty salon very happy with the healing that God had performed in my life that afternoon. As soon as I entered the premises, the receptionist told me that there was a client waiting for me at the chair. It was an old homosexual colleague. When I came nearby, he said ironically, "Is it true that you have become a believer? The guys are missing you."

I did not answer. I started cutting his hair. He looked at me and asked, "So, is it true that Jesus is healing people from AIDS now?"

I was not expecting to hear that kind of question, not at this particular moment anyway. The devil is everywhere, and he heard what God had just told me during the service. That's why he was using this man to try to create doubts in my heart, so I could lose the blessing I had just received. This was the strategy used by the devil, because he knows that,

"... the one who doubts is like a wave of the sea, blown and tossed by the wind. That person should not expect to receive anything from the Lord" (James 1:6, 7).

When I finished cutting his hair, I felt dizzy and very burdened. I looked for Zaíra, but she was with another client. Then, I asked Fátima, another Christian hairdresser, to take me out of the beauty salon because I couldn't even find the way out by myself. Once we were outside, I asked Fátima to pray with me, even if she did not understand what I was going to ask God, "I prayed, 'God, please take my life. Take me to your glory, I cannot handle it anymore.'"

Fátima started crying and said, "Jorge, I do not know why you are asking for this, but when you were praying, I saw an angel come down from Heaven and dry your tears. God will give you your victory!"

This word came like a balm to my desperate heart. Once we finished, the receptionist called me to see a client, a tourist who was passing by and decided to have her hair done. When I came nearby, I heard her singing these words:

> "Covenant of the Lord
> I am with you,
> There are no more walls within me.
> I am free to love you ..."

This young woman was a servant of God who had entered the premises to bring those words to my heart. Immediately, my soul was filled with peace. Now I knew, we could talk about the things of God.

When I got home after work, I took a shower. During my shower, I kept saying, "Lord, I praise You!" And I claimed Isaiah 53:5,

> "But he was pierced for our transgressions, he was crushed for our iniquities; the punishment that brought us peace was on him, and by his wounds we are healed."

And looking at the sarcoma, I declared, "... and by His wounds I am healed!"

It was then that something supernatural happened. The towel that was hanging over the side of the shower, and a cold wind blew over my back. I felt the enemy's presence in that place, but fearlessly, I declared with God's authority, "Devil, you have hurt me and tried to enslave me, but now my life belongs to

Jesus. Go away, in Jesus' Name." Immediately, peace took over that bathroom.

AIDS is a type of illness that brings with it the spirit of death. In that moment, when I looked at the cancer, I declared the Word of God. He allowed me to feel it, but also to cast it out. The spirit of illness that was manifested went away because of the authority in the Name of Jesus, the Name that is above all names.

When I left the bathroom, the landlord came out of his room and asked me for help to take him to the hospital. He was not feeling well. He had symptoms of blurred vision and dizziness. I rushed to help him, but then I remembered I had just rebuked the spirit of illness. It went inside this man's body, who had been a believer for many years.

I told him to sit on the chair. I would not be taking him to the hospital, but I would pray for him instead. I began to rebuke the evil spirit, and instantly, to the glory of Dr. Jesus of Nazareth, he was healed.

When I woke up the following day, I remembered Sister Noemi, the old neighbor who used to tell me about Jesus during my childhood. I phoned her to let her know what God was doing in my life. While we talked, we cried together. She got so emotional that she couldn't talk anymore. Then, she passed the phone to another sister who had just arrived at her home. As soon as she took the phone, she took out a message from a small promise box that had always stayed next to the phone. She said, "My name is Eunice, but you can call me Nicinha. God asks me to tell you that He has heard your prayer. He saw your tears and He will give you the victory on the third day. The Word is in 2 Kings 20:5. My son, on the third day, you will be healed!"

The most interesting thing in all of this is that I had not spoken at all about my illness. However, God, Who knows all things, once again had used someone to confirm the healing in my life.

I kept those words in my heart, and I rejoiced with the promise of healing that God had made to me.

Chapter 6

THE GREAT WORK

"Since ancient times no one has heard, no ear has perceived, no eye has seen any God besides you, who acts on behalf of those who wait for him" (Isaiah 64:4).

Among my work colleagues, there was a man named Tony, who chose not to speak to me. However, after I gave my life to Christ, I wanted to resolve all the issues that might conflict with my spiritual growth. So, I asked God to give me the opportunity to talk with him.

One day, I went upstairs to have lunch and Tony was there alone. I went over to him and asked him to forgive me for my attitude or anything I might have said that may have offended him in the past. He told me that he had nothing against me, but he was about to lose all of his friends. He asked me to pray for him. He had just taken the HIV test and the results were taking too long in coming back to him. The clinic had set the dates for the results to be back on December 17. From that day on, I earned his friendship, and I started praying for him.

God had made me a promise, and He put a deadline on my healing to be in three days. I started the countdown, and every day that went by, even though I still had the sarcoma in my body, I believed more in what He said than what I saw. When I woke up that Sunday morning, the third day, I didn't feel any more pain in my kidneys, and to the glory of Jesus, the cancer was gone!

Miracles cannot be explained; they have to be lived. Whenever people prophesied in relation to what God would do in my life, the most interesting thing was that they all said it would be a "great work." I just couldn't imagine how big it would be. When we believe, God performs miracles in our lives. Hallelujah!

Before God gives us something, He searches and proves our hearts first. Then, He blesses us according to our own actions. Until I was completely healed, I was proved in all the areas of my life so God could know my true motivation—was it to serve Him or only receive the healing?

> "Blessed is the one whom God corrects; so do not despise the discipline of the Almighty. For he wounds, but he also binds up; he injures, but his hands also heal" (Job 5:17, 18).

Many people work hard to receive a physical healing in their bodies, but they forget a crucial point—the healing of their soul. The great work of God in a man's life is not to heal him from his physical illness, but from his soulish one. This is indeed the most dangerous one because it can drive us to eternal death.

In order to dissipate any doubt about my healing, I had to prove it scientifically. I needed to do the HIV test again. I asked the doctor to prescribe a new exam for me, but he requested that I do it in a reputable laboratory—one that he chose. Fearlessly, I did the exam again on the following morning, and I waited for the results that were meant to come on January 4, 1995. Remember this date, because through this, God wanted to show something to all those in the beauty shop, mainly the homosexual ones. They would see the great difference between the ones who serve God and the ones who don't, as it is written in Malachi 3:18,

> "And you will again see the distinction between the righteous and the wicked, between those who serve God and those who do not."

I had been a slave to the homosexual lifestyle, just like they had. However, I wanted to come out of this sinful life, and that's why I repented of my ways and cried out for help. God heard me, set me free and healed me of my illness. This alone, for some people, would be impossible to happen. Is there anything impossible with God? Surely not!

I was anxiously waiting for the test results, but I was sure of the fulfillment of God's promise in my life. One night, the Lord woke me up to pray for the people in the laboratory. I felt that the enemy was working on something to confuse them. I started to pray for God to put His angels there to keep my blood sample and their staff safe, and for Him to undo any diabolical plan that would falsify my results.

On the morning of January 2, 1995, I woke up with my cell phone ringing. It was a member of the laboratory's staff. They were informing me that my exam results were already ready—two days in advance.

I left home confident of my victory, and as soon as I arrived, I realized that the devil wanted to create doubt in my heart. I heard two members of the staff talking about someone who had fainted after receiving their HIV test result. However, I ignored that and got my envelope. When I opened it, there was my victory—NEGATIVE!

Glory to God! Within the deadline, God fulfilled His promise. This was the great work that God said He would do in my life. First, to seek His kingdom and His righteousness, and all the other things would be given to us, as well. The biggest miracle that I could experience wasn't only the healing of my physical illness, but the experience of a new birth. What would I gain, if I had only experienced the healing of my physical illness and had not experienced a new life in Christ Jesus?

I left the laboratory very happy to go to my workplace. As I was entering the beauty salon, I was surprised to see my colleague Tony who was expecting me. He was worried and asked me for a favor—to go with him to the laboratory to get his HIV exam results, which had now been delayed fifteen days. I couldn't go because I had a client to see, so he went in the company of someone else.

At the beginning of the evening, Tony came back from the laboratory. He called all the colleagues to the entrance of the beauty salon. He asked everyone not to treat him badly, because his exam had tested POSITIVE. Everyone was very sad, but I started telling him that God could heal him. However, he resisted. He said he knew that God could set him free, but he enjoyed his homosexual lifestyle and that he wanted to continue living that way.

There is a time for everything under the heavens. God changed the time. He delayed Tony's results in anticipation of mine. Different results collected on the same day, so He could show that there is a difference between the ones who serve God and the ones who don't.

> "Whoever conceals their sins does not prosper, but the one who confesses and renounces them finds mercy" **(Proverbs 28:13)**.

Tony's illness quickly got worse. There were infections and soon cancer came. Even with chemotherapy, he did not get better. It was exactly as my doctor had explained to me. Not long after, he was hospitalized. I went there with my mother to visit him and to share with him the salvation message. When I saw him, he looked very bad, even though he was taking all of his medicine. He was very skinny and the cancer had spread to the rest of his body. So, without wasting a second, we told him about Jesus. Unfortunately, he rejected Him once again.

He asked me, "Why so much faith? The Bible says that faith without deeds is useless, so give me a massage."

We put some gloves on and using the olive oil that was next to his bed, my mother and I began to massage his legs. At that moment, God spoke to my heart, "If it wasn't for the Lord's mercy in my life, my mother would be massaging me, not Tony." God does not show favoritism, but we need to repent to receive His mercy.

I insisted with Tony for him to hear more about Jesus, but laughing, he said, "Ah! I know that Jesus set you free, but I like carnival, I like the world ..."

Unfortunately, he rejected LIFE and chose death. A few days later, he died. I don't know if in his last moments he received Jesus in his life or not. Everything happened so fast, but everyone in the beauty salon where I worked were witnesses of what had happened to me as opposed to what had happened to Tony.

The days went by, but the time came again for me to meet the young woman from my dream. I waited the 15-day time frame that she proposed for us to pray, and on the morning of the meeting day, I read about the meeting of Isaac and Rebecca in Genesis, chapter 24. I felt that there was a specific message there for me in verse 8,

"If the woman is unwilling to come back with you,
then you will be released from this oath of mine ..."

So I put on my best clothes and my best aftershave, and I went to work. I could hardly wait for the moment when she would come and we would decide our future.

She arrived at 3:00 p.m. My heart was beating so fast, just waiting for the moment to hear her say, "Yes." We began to talk about everything that had happened; about the way that God spoke to us and how all this was coming together. It was at that moment when she stopped and said, "Despite everything God said and showed us, I still have my free will, and I do not want to make any sort of commitment to you."

The feeling I had right then was that the world had just fallen on my head! I wasn't expecting that answer. I thought it would be the beginning of our relationship, but it was the opposite. Sadness filled my heart, and I could hear clearly the devil telling me, "Who will want you?" It was extremely frustrating, but I remembered the word that I had received that morning, "If the woman is unwilling to come back with you, then you will be released from this oath of mine!" I looked right into her eyes and said, "God prepared me for this moment by telling me that I would be released from our oath in case you would give me a negative answer. However, please know that I will never forget you."

She asked me, "Why?"

I said, "Because God Himself has directed me to meet you. When the devil was telling me that I would never love a woman, God showed you to me in a dream, and He has placed in my heart the love of a man to a woman. God called into being the things that were not."

Continuing to look into her eyes, I said, "One day, I will marry and the glory of the new house will be greater than the glory of the former house."

She said, "I don't understand how God speaks to you so clearly, since you are still a newborn Christian."

It was really difficult, but because God had prepared me for this beforehand, I felt a peace and there was no confusion at all.

This was one of the biggest faith tests I have ever

experienced, but all of it contributed to mature my feelings and heal my emotions. God wanted to ensure to me that I could, indeed, feel attracted to a woman. Now that this was so, I had to be careful not to sin against God. I knew he was preparing a wife for me, someone who was pure and very special. The Lord told me that she would be mature in the faith, someone who would believe in the miracle that He had done in my life. Many people abandon Jesus and lose the best gift God has for them. But I remained faithful while I waited for her.

Every day that went by, I was losing the passion for my profession. God told me that my time at the beauty salon was ending, and He would move me out of there. I just couldn't wait to leave because my heart wasn't there anymore; I couldn't bear the work environment—the talks, etc. Believe it or not, I gave testimony to everyone about my healing; this was my duty as a Christian. Some were saying that I had gone crazy, but I obeyed the order I had received in Ezekiel, chapter 3. Even if they were not listening, I had to talk about Jesus. I didn't want blood on my hands, if they died living a sinful life, and I hadn't told them about Him. At no time or for any reason did I run away; I tolerated all the humiliation. My work colleagues had already seen what God had done in my life. It was time to leave.

When I was praying one morning, I heard God's voice telling me, "Today is your last day there." So, I arrived at work on that day with this certainty. Once there, the manager very shyly told me not to see any clients before speaking to the owner. I smiled and said, "Today is my last day!"

The receptionist did not understand my comment and asked

me how I knew about this. I replied by saying that God had told me about this. Now, everyone became frightened.

Later on, the owner called me into her office and confirmed what I already knew. She said, "I have no complaints about you. Your clients love you, but your time here is over."

I smiled and said, "I thank God for your life, because it was in this beauty salon that I had a remarkable experience I will never forget. I started working here just like my colleagues, but I had an experience with God."

A bit shy, she said, "Who knows; we may meet again?"

I left the beauty salon in God's time. I soon received an invitation to be a sales representative for an Argentinian cosmetic company, but this was only a strategy of God's to fill up my time while I was slowly being removed from the type of environment I used to work in.

During this time, I began to give my testimony of Christ and of His work in my life. I told people about this God, Who had healed me, transformed me and set me free. I became a missionary, living by faith and experiencing the supernatural provision of God in my life.

Chapter 7

THE FULFILLMENT OF THE PROMISE

"The LORD God said, 'It is not good for the man to be alone.
I will make a helper suitable for him'"
(Genesis 2:18).

I was single and young, and I had a calling to minister the Word of God. It was a perfect combination, for many young women came to hear me, which allowed them to be potential candidates as my future wife. However, I had a promise from God about my marriage, and I was willing to wait for the right person to come along, even if it meant conquering my own anxiety or facing other people's disbelief.

I was always giving my testimony about what God had done in my life. Many still doubted, asking me who this woman would be, since she had not yet appeared to me. The only thing that God had told me was that she would be very pretty, pure and someone who knew His power. Even close friends doubted that God had really healed me, and I could be attracted to a woman. Unfortunately, many wanted to see it in order to believe it. But the Word says,

"… blessed are those who have not seen and yet

have believed" (John 20:29).

I have faced many spiritual battles, but the promise was fulfilled. However, at all times, God was preparing me to receive my blessing—my beloved wife, Hérica Simaya.

HÉRICA'S JOURNEY

On September 9, 1978, in Almenara, Minas Gerais, Brazil, a beautiful girl named Hérica Simaya Pires Silva was born. She was the youngest of eight siblings. When she was seven years old, her parents moved to Rondônia, Brazil. Her first visit to a Christian service happened through the invitation of one neighbor.

During the worship time, a song touched her heart:
"I want you to value what you have,
You are someone
Very important to God ...
You are valuable!
The Holy Spirit is moving in you ..."

Through this song, God spoke to her heart, and when she was ten years old, she had a personal experience with the Lord, which resulted in surrendering her life to Him. Despite the fact that she was still very young, she was sure about her decision to live for Christ. Three years later, she was baptized. But there was much controversy with her family because of her decision. Hérica and her family did not share the same faith. Luke 14:26 says,

"If anyone comes to me and does not hate father

and mother, wife and children, brothers and sisters—yes, even their own life—such a person cannot be my disciple."

At the age of fifteen, she moved to Ilhéus with her family. She started going to an evangelical church with some brothers in the faith where she developed her ministry by singing, dancing and serving the Lord. No one in her family had converted to Christ yet, but she knew that her prayers for her family's salvation were going before God. She knew God would find a way to save them.

Everything was going well until one night. Suddenly she woke up. To her surprise, all her family members were standing by her bed, crying. She asked, "What happened? Why are you all here by my bed?" Nobody would tell her anything. They thought it would be better if she didn't know that she had just had a horrendous epileptic seizure.

Every night, the crisis became worse, so her parents decided to take her to the doctor. After many exams, it was detected that there was something wrong in her brain, but there were no other available resources in the city for a more precise diagnosis. They were then instructed by the doctor to take her to a more sophisticated and equipped medical center.

During this time, she continued to actively serve the Lord. Despite all the difficulties she was going through, she never questioned God about the reason for her illness. She knew that God could use this situation to touch the heart of her family members. Then, the situation really started to change.

One evening, when Hérica came back from school, she was surprised to find out that her mother was at the house of a Christian neighbor. She was actually praying for her. She was filled with joy because her mother had never had any kind of a relationship with the evangelical community. However, because of the gravity of Hérica's situation, Mrs. Erenice decided to seek help.

As soon as she entered her neighbor's house, she found all of them were praying, including her mother. However, just as Hérica joined the group to pray, she started to not feel well; she wanted to open her eyes, but she could not. A few seconds later, she fainted. It was another epileptic seizure. These seizures always happened during the night, but this one was different. Also, the seizures would usually last for five minutes, but Hérica remained unconscious for over half an hour. Everyone prayed, but nothing happened.

Then, one brother in the faith told Mrs. Erenice that many people had already prayed for Hérica, but nothing happened. He continued by telling her that if she made a covenant with God, and asked Him to bring her life back, then the seizures would stop. Troubled by seeing her daughter that way, she kneeled down and said, "Lord Jesus, I give you my life; please, bring my daughter back."

Instantly, and in a miraculous way, Hérica opened her eyes and got up. She asked what had happened. During the time of the seizure, she had an experience with God. She saw her body on the floor and her spirit being taken away; she also saw her mother and the other people who were in the room asking God not to take her away. She then asked God not to take her away, because her parents had not yet come to Christ. It was then that she saw her spirit come back into her body and she regained consciousness again.

Science admits the existence of a human encounter called a near death experience. This is where people may go through supernatural experiences. We know that we are a spirit, we have a soul and we live in a body. What Hérica had experienced was definitely something in the supernatural, since she left her body but was still able to see what was happening. After that episode, she did not have any seizures for four months, she stopped taking the medicine, and she began to sleep peacefully.

Mrs. Erenice was really criticized for making a decision to serve Christ. Even her husband was upset and left home for three days because of it. Her sister accused her of betraying Mary, who's considered a saint in their religion, but she replied by saying that Jesus had healed her daughter.

However, the time had come for Mrs. Erenice to have her faith tested by God, to confirm whether she believed or not in the prayer she had spoken on her daughters behalf. Then, Mrs. Erenice's sister asked her, "What if the epileptic seizures come back?"

She replied, "If they come back, so be it."

The Bible teaches us to ask God about things, with faith, never doubting,

> "... because the one who doubts is like a wave of the sea, blown and tossed by the wind. That person should not expect to receive anything from the

Lord" (James 1:6, 7).

Doubt is a weapon that our enemy uses to steal our blessings. Therefore, whenever God does something or promises you something, do not doubt, because He is faithful!

Mrs. Erenice failed the test because she doubted, and the seizures came back even stronger. She then took Hérica to Campinas, São Paulo, where she could be treated in the medical center of the University of Campinas, which is one of the best hospitals in Latin America.

Hérica's family was going through a very difficult financial period, and they could not afford the costs—transportation, exams, medications and medical appointments. However, with the help of some brothers in Christ, they managed to gather some money and arrive at Campinas. But there was another obstacle—undergoing all the necessary procedures to treat that illness.

After a more precise exam, it was diagnosed that Hérica had a brain tumor that could cause her to die instantly. Since it was found in a very dangerous area of the brain, surgery could cause traumatic affects.

Also, in order for the operation to happen, she would need to get on a waiting list that could take more than six months. Hérica did not have this time; her life was already at risk. Her family did not have the means to pay for a private surgery, so the only solution was to rely on the solidarity of their friends.

Sometimes, we find ourselves in certain types of situations, which drive us to think that God has forgotten about us. It's like going up a staircase and the stairs behind us disappear as soon as we walk up. It is impossible to go back. Our only solution is to keep going up, believing that God will give us the victory because,

> "... He who began a good work in you will carry it on to completion until the day of Christ Jesus" (Philippians 1:6).

Hérica was depending on God to supernaturally provide a solution for her problem.

One day, her brother, who used to work in a beauty salon in Campinas, was approached by one of her clients. She asked, "Geraldo, how is your sister? Has she had her surgery yet?"

He replied very sadly, "No. She is still on a long list for the surgery. Also, we don't have the money we need to pay for a private surgery. We are really worried ..."

Her response then came as a great surprise to him. She said, "I work in the neurological center at the University of Campinas. Ask your mother and sister to meet me tomorrow morning at the hospital entrance. I will organize everything for the surgery."

Hallelujah! God is faithful! Many people were praying and God began to act. He had opened a new door, and He was meeting all of Hérica's needs—just like He meets our needs today. God cares about you, even the small details of your life. Sometimes, it may seem like a long time, but whenever God orders His angels to come and work on your behalf, then all the doors open up.

The next morning, Hérica and her mother met that lady. She did all the exams that were needed and they organized everything for the surgery. In few days, Hérica was going to have her surgery done.

The surgery happened on the morning of July 2, 1997. They shaved Hérica's head, and she was taken to the surgery room. While she waited for the surgery to begin, she prayed to God in the corridor, "Lord Jesus, I put my life in Your hands; if I am to live, so be it; if I am to die, so be it, as I will be with You in glory." She started to sing,

"My God is the God of the impossible,
Jehovah-jireh, the great El Shaddai,
Who opened the Red Sea and let His people pass,
God that made water gush out from the rock ..."

She kept saying that He healed the blind, the paralyzed, the mute ... her heart was full of faith. One of the nurses, watching Hérica sing, tried to comfort Mrs. Erenice by telling her that her daughter was at peace, explaining that she had seen her singing a very beautiful song. It didn't even seem as though she was about to go in for an operation. What the nurse did not know was that the God of the impossible was strengthening Hérica and giving her the courage to handle this storm.

Before the surgery began, the surgeon asked someone to tell Hérica's family that if she survived, she could be blind, mute, deaf or disabled. Her health condition was really serious and delicate. Also, the tumor was in a very deep position in the brain. The surgery was supposed to take around twelve hours and she could remain in a coma for many days.

Mrs. Erenice was very nervous as you can imagine! She did not know if she should call her family, or if she should call her brothers in the faith so they could pray for Hérica. However, through every moment, God never lost control of this situation.

God can make a miracle in many different ways, and He may use many things to achieve this. The Bible shows us that Jesus performed many miracles and in many different ways. At different times he healed two blind people. It was only one of them that He told to go and wash their eyes in the Pool of Siloam. To the other one He said, "Your faith has healed you." God does everything exactly the way He wants it. He was creating the miracle in Hérica's life in a very special way.

It seemed that time just stood still, but after six hours of surgery, the doctor came out to speak with Mrs. Erenice. Smiling, he said, "Congratulations, the surgery was magnificent! It was the best surgery of my life!"

Actually, it wasn't the doctor who did the surgery; he was only a tool in God's hands. Jesus Christ was, in fact, the One Who did the surgery in Hérica! He is the Doctor of all doctors, and He is a specialist in all lost causes.

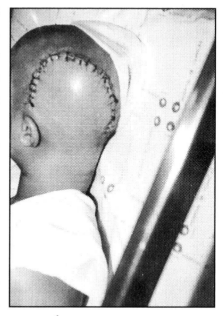

HÉRICA'S SURGERY

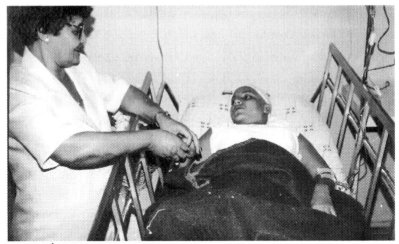

HÉRICA AND HER MOTHER AFTER THE SURGERY.

Moments after the surgery was over, Hérica heard her mother anxiously calling her name, "Hérica! Hérica!"

She said, "Hello mother."

Mrs. Erenice then began to glorify God, saying, "Jesus healed my daughter! She can hear, she can talk, she can see ..."

In that hospital, God did a miracle in Hérica's life. Her recovery was exceptional, and in a few days, she was ready to go back home without any side effects. She went back to the hospital one year later. The doctors confirmed she was totally healed. They were speechless when it came to her quick recovery. The doctors told her she would live a completely normal life. She did not need to take any more medicine; she could work, marry, have children and do all of her normal daily activities. GOD IS FAITHFUL! JEHOVAH-RAPHA, THE GOD WHO HEALS!

I FINALLY MEET MY WIFE

I always believed that God would give me a wife who had already experienced His power. For anyone to marry me, it would have to be someone who would not doubt what God had done in my life.

In 1997, I decided to spend my holidays in Ilhéus to rest from the battles I had gone through at work. My aunt Vera used to attend a Christian service, and one Sunday evening, I decided to accompany her. Just after I arrived, a very pretty woman caught my eye. She was smiling as she entered the place with her fiancé. She had short hair, which was still wet. It was the first time I had seen her. Later that night, a mutual friend introduced us, but we didn't have time to talk or get to know each other.

One morning, while I was praying in my bedroom, I heard a sweet voice calling my aunt, "Vera, Vera!"

I quickly left my room to see who it was. To my surprise, it was Hérica, the same girl from the church service. She was very sad. She had come here to talk to my aunt, but she wasn't at home. She came in anyway, and we talked. Amidst the conversation, she told me that three months before her wedding, her fiancé decided to break up with her. She was suffering and feeling rejected.

After listening to her, I tried to comfort her by mentioning the Scripture from John 13:7,

> "Jesus replied, 'You do not realize now what I am doing, but later you will understand.'"

I told her that God had saved her from a bad decision and

that He had a very special plan reserved for her. So we prayed and she left.

I knew there was a purpose for that meeting, especially because my aunt wasn't home. We talked and we got to know each other better. I felt nothing for her at that time because I only wanted to help her overcome this frustration.

As soon as my aunt got back home, I told her what had happened. I also made one comment, "She is really pretty! If God gave her to me, I would marry her."

God acknowledged those words that came out of my mouth in the spiritual world, "If God gave her to me, I would marry her."

Every promise has its appointed time until God fulfills it. In Ecclesiastes 3:1, 11 says,

> "There is a time for everything, and a season for every activity under the heavens ... He has made everything beautiful in its time."

Whenever God promises something, He fulfills it, even if it takes a long time to do it.

The waiting period between the promise that is made and its fulfillment is a time that God uses to do a work in our lives, to enable us to believe and receive what He has promised us. When it comes to marriage, God prepares both hearts for this commitment.

In order to understand this better, I will make an analogy with preparing a cake. To make a cake, the ingredients are mixed one by one in the correct order, and then it is put in the oven to bake. Only then, will the cake be ready for eating. If we remove the cake from the oven before it is ready, surely it will not taste good. Part of it will still be raw. On the other hand, if we remove it after the correct time, it will be burnt. It is the same for us. If we rush or allow our own anxieties to control us, we may harm ourselves by not receiving from God what He had prepared for us.

Even though, at this point, I might not have been a Christian for a very long time, I have already seen a lot of damage caused to young people by their rush to get married. Many say they are following a direction from God, but they end up breaking many of God's principles. They forget about the blessing of their parents, the obedience to the authorities constituted by God upon their lives and the biblical standards for a Christian marriage. In addition to these, people forget that in order to marry someone, they must have spiritual knowledge and a stable emotional structure to engage in such a commitment.

Many people also believe that a marriage is summed up in the joy of having sexual relations. They forget that it is a very serious covenant, with its final aim to cooperate with God's eternal purposes for their lives. Only death must end this covenant that is made between a man and a woman during the matrimonial vows.

> "It is better not to make a vow than to make one and not fulfill it. Do not let your mouth lead you into sin. And do not protest to the temple messenger, 'My vow was a mistake.' Why should God be

angry at what you say and destroy the work of your hands? Much dreaming and many words are meaningless. Therefore fear God" (Ecclesiastes 5:5-7).

After the break up, Hérica decided to move to São Paulo. Following her frustration, she didn't want to be married anymore, but to live only for Jesus. She always dreamed of becoming an airline stewardess. So she started to seek her dream by enrolling in an aviation school. With the help of some sisters in the faith, she paid for a very expensive course at EDAPA School, where she impressed people because of her height, attitude, beauty and education. She successfully completed nearly all the stages, only missing a final interview to receive her license. The interview would be a crucial moment, because she knew that she would be questioned about her health, and as a servant of God, she could not lie about it.

Before the interview, Hérica prayed, "Lord, if this is your will for me, please let them pass me and give me my license." At this time, her hair had already grown out again, hiding the scar on her head. She also did not need medicine anymore, because she had no more epileptic seizures. However, she was questioned if she had ever gone through a surgery or had experienced any epileptic seizures. She replied, "Yes, I have. I went through a surgery four years ago, but I am fine now."

The doctor then told her, "Unfortunately, I cannot give you your license because you are not fit for this kind of job. In spite of all the medical exams being normal, I cannot go ahead because of the surgery you had."

Frustration is part of our process in maturing. When God says, "No," to us, we must mature in all areas. Many times, when a father says, "No," to a son, it is because he does not want him to suffer. He only wants the best for him; the father wishes that the son wouldn't have to go through anything that he will regret in the future. When God said, "No," to Hérica, she wasn't happy about it. However, even though she cried at that moment, she understood that God had answered her prayer. He had the best reserved for her future.

> "However, as it is written: 'What no eye has seen, what no ear has heard, and what no human mind has conceived'—the things God has prepared for those who love him—" (1 Corinthians 2:9).

When God opens one door, nobody can shut it, but if He shuts it, then who can open it? Hallelujah! He is amazing! He is in control of all things, and His eyes are everywhere!

Four years after I met Hérica, I decided to talk to her. I phoned my family in Ilhéus, and I was surprised to learn that she was in Campinas, studying to become an airline stewardess. Her sister, Jane gave me her phone number, and I got in touch with her that same day. I realized that she was happy when she heard my voice, and once again, she opened her heart to me by telling me about her frustration of not being given her license.

I tried to help her by saying that God didn't want her working for any man, but God wanted her collaborating with his Kingdom, giving testimony of what He had done in her life. Then, we prayed and ended our conversation, but we talked again on other occasions.

In June, 2002, I was already a missionary and a leader of a church in Salvador. I organized a church retreat in conjunction with a Christian community in Ilhéus. To my surprise, as soon as we arrived there, I bumped into Hérica, who was a member of the worship team. As I think back on those days, I remember what a big blessing they were to all of us. I could barely speak to Hérica because I was leading a group of more than fifty people. At the end of the retreat, we had a chance to talk. She told me that she had moved back to Ilhéus, she was now working in a health clinic, and continued on about all the things that had happened in her life with Christ. I realized she was waiting on the Lord.

I had the chance to meet her father, who was a very happy and simple man, and to see her mother again. It was a great time, and my heart began to give me signs of something that I didn't know how to acknowledge.

Because we were all together, I took the opportunity to ask Hérica's parents and her Pastor, for permission to allow her to come to Salvador to give her testimony of the miracle God had done in her life. One month later, she came and shared with the church about her healing experience. After that, one sister in the faith came to pray with us and told us the message, which can be found in the Book of Acts. In this Bible text, it speaks about one vision, one purpose and one ministry. She recommended we pray together for twenty-one days so God would reveal if it were His plan for Hérica and I to get married.

We spent those days praying and fasting, but nothing happened. When the twenty-one days ended, I called Hérica and asked her if she felt anything for me. A bit shy, she told me that she hadn't felt anything, yet. Then God drove me back to Ilhéus to speak to her parents. As soon as I arrived there, I met with them and asked for their permission and blessing to marry their daughter. They gave me their blessing, but Hérica still had to accept.

When I saw her, I took her by the hand. Instantly, a very strong feeling rose up in my heart. When I left her home, I already had the engagement date arranged. I did not go there just to start a relationship with her; I wanted to marry her.

In the Bible we only see engagements and marriages. There are no other types of relationships. Today, many young Christian couples end up harming the holiness of God in their lives. They get too involved in a physical and emotional intimacy that should only be achieved within the marriage. It is undeniable that whenever someone kisses another person on the mouth, it is a preparation for something more to happen.

On the other hand, when kissing does not take place, the desire to do so may generate unclean or sexual thoughts that can pollute one's mind.

> "Marriage should be honored by all, and the marriage bed kept pure, for God will judge the adulterer and all the sexually immoral"
> (Hebrews 13:4).

In August, a group of young people, which Hérica was a part of, came to Salvador for a theater presentation. I took the opportunity to surprise her. I bought the wedding rings, and I introduced her to my brothers in the faith as my future wife. It was a day of great joy for my brothers in the faith. They had been praying a long time for God to send me a wife. Ultimately, how could I lead the people and give advice to couples if I was still single? Many people cried when they witnessed one more of God's promises being fulfilled in my life. When a member of the body is honored, the whole body is also honored.

We organized our engagement for September 7, 2002. Then, we got engaged in the presence of our families, and we waited anxiously for the big day. It was three months between our engagement and the wedding, exactly like God told me it would be.

JORGE AND HÉRICA'S ENGAGEMENT PHOTO

As a missionary, I could not afford to pay for a wedding, but God soon arranged everything we needed. He touched people's heart to increase the amount of the offerings I had been receiving. God used so many people to bless us, from the wedding party to the honeymoon. We were honored and felt like a prince and a princess. God is really faithful to fulfill all of His promises in our lives!

On December 7, 2002, we were married at the main Assembly of God Church in Salvador. It was quite the party with over 600 guests. Many came to witness God's great power. They could see that God can do much more than what we ask or think, according to His power.

WEDDING PHOTOS

WEDDING PHOTOS

Obviously, until the big day, there were many attempts of the enemy to frustrate the fulfillment of God's promise in our lives. However, as already mentioned, when God says, "Yes" to something, nothing else can go against it. The Word says that the gates of Hades will not overcome it.

The glory of this present house will be greater than the glory of the former house. Even after being rejected by who I thought was the woman of my dreams, I didn't stop believing. God is faithful to fulfill His promises. Even if the promise takes a long time, it will be fulfilled. God is not a man that He should lie. When He promises something, He fulfills it; He did it for me!

Our honeymoon was amazing! It was a totally different experience than anything I had ever had. It was incomparably better. Even after living for many years in sin, God gifted me with a virgin wife. He taught us and enabled us for everything. Where sin increased, grace increased all the more (Romans 5:20), because God forgot all my sins. Hallelujah! Jesus helped me conquer all the fears that the devil tried to put in my mind, deceiving me for all those years when I was a slave to the homosexual lifestyle and when I thought that I would never have any pleasure with a woman.

Sex is a big blessing from God to mankind, something He reserves for us to enjoy after we get married. But the devil, who is the father of all lies, tries to deceive people by making them slaves to sin. However, the truth has set me free. Jesus, the Truth, convicted me to repent from my sins of living as a homosexual and showed me that I needed to be healed. I was blessed with a great victory—my freedom from sin and from the devil. Hallelujah!

If you want to be free, Jesus can set you free! He wants to and He can change your life, too. Do not keep being deceived by the devil's lies. Ask God for help. In a sinful life, there is no peace or joy, but only glimpses of pleasure and a great feeling of guilt.

On December 28, 2002, I was anointed as the Pastor, and I became the Pastor of the same group of brothers in the faith. Even before my

PASTOR LUÍS BEING ANOINTED

marriage, they believed in what God had done in my life, healing me and setting me free from the homosexual world.

Before I got married, the Lord told me I would be the father of a boy. After four months of marriage, we received great news. Our first son, Isaac, was on his way. One more of God's promises being fulfilled in our lives. On January 9, 2004, Isaac Luís was born. And two years later, on September 21, 2006, we had our second son, Samuel. They are both blessings from the Lord and the proof of God's faithfulness.

Contrary to what it may seem, it hasn't been easy for us to come this far. As I already mentioned, between the promise being made and its fulfillment, there was a long road that needed to be travelled. There were many battles, difficulties and harassments. Only God knows how hard this journey has been, but it has been a rewarding one as well.

In order to have His plan fulfilled in us, God transformed our lives and enabled us to do His work. It is worth believing, persevering and resisting temptation. Like an athlete, we run

THE SANTOS FAMILY

toward the victory, and to achieve it, we need to go through tough training, and give up many things along the way that can and will hold us back. Our reward is an incorruptible crown, which has already been reserved for us. We have this promise and our victory is already secure. Faithful is the One Who made the promise.

> "Let us hold unswervingly to the hope we profess, for he who promised is faithful" (Hebrews 10:23).

> "The Lord is not slow in keeping his promise, as some understand slowness. Instead he is patient with you, not wanting anyone to perish, but everyone to come to repentance" (2 Peter 3:9).

If you have never surrendered your life to Jesus, I pray that after reading this book, you have heard the voice of the Holy Spirit speaking to your heart, and you have felt a desire within you to lay down any areas of sin you have in your life.

I invite you now to pray, repenting from your sins and giving your life to Christ.

> "If you declare with your mouth, 'Jesus is Lord,' and believe in your heart that God raised him from the dead, you will be saved. For it is with your heart that you believe and are justified, and it is with your mouth that you profess your faith and are saved" (Romans 10: 9, 10).

Wherever you are, ask the Holy Spirit to guide you in the following prayer:

"Lord Jesus, I _____ recognize that I am a sinner, and today, I repent of my sins. I invite You to enter my heart. Please, forgive my sins, wash me with Your blood and give me Your salvation. I give up all the covenants I had made with the kingdom of darkness. Lord Jesus, I give up all evil practices and I break up any covenant made with the devil, through the power in the blood and name of Jesus. Amen"

If you have prayed with an open heart, know that God will begin to act in your life. Start praying to God. Acquire a Bible for yourself if you don't have one yet, because that is the main tool God uses to talk to mankind.

> "All Scripture is God-breathed and is useful for teaching, rebuking, correcting and training in righteousness, so that the servant of God may be thoroughly equipped for every good work"
> (2 Timothy 3:16, 17).

Do not stay alone, but seek the help of a Christian church and submit yourself to the spiritual authority of someone who is obedient to God.

Do not forget—God has a great work for your life!

Chapter 8

THERE IS HOPE FOR THE BROKEN

The love of Christ compels us. His love for us can't be measured—it is endless. Nothing can stop the supernatural flow of God's love. It is impossible to describe with words what God has done in our lives. When I was abandoned, He gave me shelter and a family; when I was hurt, He healed me; when I was dying, He gave me life; when I was a slave of the devil and sin, He set me free. Hallelujah! How great is His love for us!

Our God is almighty. He makes the lonely person dwell in a family; He is the Way for the lost; He is the Loaf for the hungry; He is the Light for the blind; He is the Father for the orphan; and He is the Doctor for the sick. He can meet any need.

God has been using every necessary resource to help me fulfill my mission on Earth. He put good people in my path to help me fight against the darkness of hell. Through prayers, many people helped me walk in the faith. In the moments I could not find a way out, He showed me a way.

The secret of a prosperous life can be found in Jesus. All the good things that happened in my life could only take place because of the attitude I took—repentance, which is a change of an internal attitude and a change of thoughts. In Acts 2:38, it says,

"Repent and be baptized, every one of you, in the name of Jesus Christ for the forgiveness of your sins. And you will receive the gift of the Holy Spirit."

The greatest of all miracles is the new birth. It is moving from the kingdom of darkness to the Kingdom of God. When we start seeking God's Kingdom first and His Justice, then everything else will be added to us.

Today, we live in difficult days, full of false prophets, masters and pastors. Another gospel has been spread in the world that was not the gospel preached by Jesus and the apostles. However, the world has also been experiencing revivals and miracles, like the ones written in this book. God has been raising a generation of courageous prophets—men and women—who have been carrying their own crosses, giving up their own lives, in order to be true disciples of the Master Jesus and following Him. Amidst a world full of non-believers, God asks us, "Will I find faith on Earth?"

Faith is the key to victory and without it we cannot please God. However, He has been manifesting His power in our weaknesses, showing us that even though we are sinners, His grace will increase all the more for the ones who receive it. I have been justified and sanctified by God, and I will be glorified in Christ Jesus, Hallelujah!

Chapter 9

FINAL WORDS

"Those who cleanse themselves from the latter will be instruments for special purposes, made holy, useful to the Master and prepared to do any good work" (2 Timothy 2:21).

I would like to express my gratitude to God for one more of His promises, which was fulfilled in my life. That promise is having this book published in the U.S. It was a promise He made to me many years ago, and despite all the difficulties I've encountered, nothing could stop Him from acting in my favor.

The first difficulty I had was my Visa Application to the U.S. It was denied eleven times since 1994. My first Visa Application happened before I met Christ, and the other ten happened afterwards.

I praise the Lord for my wife, who always gave me the support and encourages me not to give up; otherwise, I would have already given up in 2007. That year, during my interview at the consulate, the agent treated me in a cold and rude manner. She told me it would be impossible for me to get a Visa, especially after a history of ten unsuccessful Visa Applications. I tried to present my argument by explaining that my two sons—

Isaac and Samuel, age three and one respectively, would stay in Brazil at the time with my aunt, while I was going to visit an American Christian Church in Boston. Unconvinced, she told me that the Brazilian people don't think anything about leaving their own children behind in order to go to the U.S. Then she ended the interview and a member of the security invited me to leave the consulate. When my wife saw how sad I was, she told me, "Now I know that God will grant you this Visa, because when something is impossible for man, God starts moving to make it become possible."

There have been many trips, expenses, taxes and frustrations, but in 2014 at the American Embassy in Brasilia, God used an angel to transform what was impossible to become possible. As soon as the interview began, a member of their staff asked me, "Ten unsuccessful Visa Applications; is that right? What are you doing here? What has changed in your life since the last time you came to see us?" I tried to explain. I waited for one hour with my family. Then, suddenly, another person came around to where we were. She started talking to the other member of the staff who was interviewing us. At one point in the conversation, they excused themselves and switched off the microphone. They didn't want us to hear what they were saying. After a few minutes, the lady left the cubicle and the agent started doing something on the computer. She didn't say a word. Then she asked my wife, Hérica, "What do you do in Brazil?"

Hérica replied, "I am a Christian Missionary and my husband's partner."

We waited again for quite a while. Then she told us, "Alright, your Visa has been granted. Enjoy your trip!"

We left the American Embassy, crying and saying, "God is faithful!"

Once again, we learned that there is a preparation time between the promise that is made and its fulfillment. Our enemy tried to frustrate God's plans in our lives, in spite of God's promise.

My first prayer when I arrived in the U.S. was, "God, please keep my heart and eyes safe so that nothing I see here can steal the treasure that exists within me—JESUS."

Once there, I went to visit the place that was promised to me years before, Christ For The Nations Institute in Dallas, Texas, where I will one day be studying. However, because it was a man who promised that to me, it did not happen. Man fails, but God never fails. God took me to America in a supernatural way; only God knows how long I waited to see this promise fulfilled in our lives. I entered this country holding God's hands, as He has the keys to open or to close any door. When He opens one door, nobody can shut it, and when He shuts it, nobody can open it. Hallelujah!

My ministerial journey has always been in Brazil, ever since I gave my life to Christ in 1995. As soon as I received the miracle in my body and soul, I started proclaiming this miracle. I had received a word from God that wherever I went, He would use me in His Name to heal and transform lives. Very quickly, I became a travelling missionary for God, even without the support of any church. God provided me with everything, including clothes, food and transportation. Wherever I went, He created miracles.

The first place where I gave my testimony was in a meeting called Hosanna Brasil, at the First Baptist Church of Brazil in Salvador. There, I spoke about how Jesus saved me and healed me from my sickness. On that day, many people gave their lives to Christ after hearing my testimony. From that moment on, I received many invitations to attend Christian events, churches, universities and schools. I travelled around many cities, giving my testimony of what God had done in my life.

In addition, God entrusted me with a church to take care of that has been meeting together now for fourteen years. We meet in an auditorium in Salvador. This church was not founded from another church split, which is somewhat the norm here, but it was started in a house with ten people, who were motivated by five young people, who invited me to celebrate a Christian service in their home. Slowly, God sent other people until we began to meet in this auditorium in January, 2000. This meeting was first known as "Meeting God," but then it was officially registered as Ministry Ágape.

I saw God do many great things during this time. On one occasion, a young woman tried to kill herself by setting her own body on fire. She was admitted to a hospital, and when I arrived there to pray for her, the nurse asked me to not stay too long. She had a serious infection and her life was at risk. When I entered the room, God gave me a Word from Ezekiel 37, the valley of dry bones. Then He said to me, "I (God) will grow flesh, skin, bones and tendons." Soon I realized that God was giving her a word of hope, and even with all her frailty, she managed to hear what I had read. Then I prayed for her, I anointed her, and I prophesied over her life that she would come out of that place and she would survive.

A few months later, I received a phone call from that young woman telling me what God had done for her. She told me that one-day, following my visit, she was sent to the surgery room where they were going to amputate her right arm. However, when the doctors removed the bandage, they asked, "Do you believe in miracles?"

She replied, "I do!"

Then, the doctors said, "This is exactly what has happened. Your veins were restored; we will no longer have to cut off your arm."

At that moment, she remembered what God had told her the day before when I visited her.

I also remember a man I met when I was volunteering in a hospital in Salvador for patients who had AIDS. When I arrived at the hospital's reception area, I needed the name of a patient to get access to the ward. Naturally, it was a restricted area. However, I didn't know anyone's name. When the receptionist asked for a name, I heard a name being whispered in my ears. I replied with certainty, "EDNEI SANTOS."

The receptionist then said, "Fine."

Once I had access to the area, it was visible that many people there needed prayer, a word of faith and hope. I prayed for a few young people who were in critical condition, and many of them received Jesus in their lives at the last minute. I had the opportunity to pray for a man named Daniel, and after preaching to him about Daniel in the lion's den, the man surrendered his life to Christ just before he died. Regardless, I was certain of Daniel's salvation.

I was leaving that place when I remembered to ask the nurse about Ednei Santos, the name God had whispered in my ear in the hospital reception area. She directed me to a young man at the end of the corridor. I came close and called his name. He was surprised, and he asked me who had given his name to me. I said, "Jesus." Then, I told him how his name was whispered to me. I told him about Jesus' love for him, and God's purpose in taking me to that hospital. I shared about my healing experience, and then, I invited him to pray with me. Ednei said, "Yes." We prayed right there. God gave me a word for him that he would leave that place and that God would give him a family. I also told him that his parents would come to look for him soon.

I gave him my word that I would come back with a Bible for him. At the end of the following week, I went back with the present I had promised. When I saw him, I realized he was happy, and quickly he invited me to his room. There were a few things he wanted to tell me. He reminded me of the prayer we had prayed the week before—about what I had told him by the Holy Spirit about his parents and his health.

He said that he had been having a high temperature for quite a while, which was due to a bacterial infection that the doctors couldn't get rid of from his body. However, that night, the fever went away. Also, he told me that the following morning, his parents, who he hadn't seen for two years because he had left home without telling them where he was going, came to see him. In addition, he told me that he had acquired the AIDS virus after he had been with a hooker.

This young man's parents, who were extremely worried about him, decided to come to Salvador to look for him. After looking for him in prisons and psychiatric institutions, they decided to go to that hospital, where they found out there was a man there with the same name as their son. The nurse said to him, "Ednei, you have a visitor today!"

That day, Ednei saw his parents and sister again, and experienced God's promise being fulfilled in his life. A few weeks later, he was allowed to leave the hospital. After a few years, his total recovery was confirmed and he learned about his miraculous recovery from that sickness. This fact caused much confusion within the hospital staff members. However, it only took a few results from the exams that made it to be certified—this man was now healed. His test results proved it when they came back, "negative" for HIV.

I was the leader at the "Casa da Criança" (Children House), a governmental entity named FUNDAC that cared for the unwanted children and adolescents who were victims of abuse. Here I had the opportunity to share my testimony with them. I told them about how God took care of me, despite the fact that my mother had abandoned me and the name of my father wasn't even on my birth certificate. I also heard their tragic stories, and took some of them to my house for a day to provide them with the love and care they always wanted and needed. It was a beautiful work, and it produced much fruit for the Kingdom of God.

I also coordinated a work for recovering drug addicts in a city that was close to where I lived. There were more than one hundred people, including adults, youngsters and the elderly, who were addicted and highly dangerous. I had remarkable experiences there.

I remember the day when a psychic patient tried to rebel against me. He threw away my cell phone so I wasn't able to communicate. When I noticed what had happened, I asked the interns who had taken my phone, but nobody said anything. They feared this rebel's reaction. Then we all gathered to pray. I asked God loudly, "GOD, PLEASE SHOW ME WHERE MY CELL PHONE IS!"

Following that, I told them, "God is going to show us where it is." I then ordered some of them to go out and look for it, while I stayed with the others praying. Suddenly, one of the interns came back with a wet cell phone in his hands. He told us that he had heard the ring tone and was able to find it. Everybody in that place could see God was moving!

I couldn't forget either when God had used me as a counselor to help a couple restore their marriage. At the beginning of my ministry, I had instructed this couple, who had recently converted to Christ, about the way they were living as a man and woman. They had a son, and they had lived together for years, even though they weren't married. They wanted to please God in such a way that they quickly got married and began to walk with Christ. A few years later, the wife decided to work to help increase the household income. She started to work in a market, and soon, some jealous conflicts appeared.

One day, the husband came home very distressed. He suspected his wife was cheating on him with her manager. I tried to calm him down, telling him that it could be a misunderstanding and for him to avoid arguments and divorce. Instead of listening to me, he hired a private detective to follow her to end his doubts. At the end of the investigation, it was confirmed that the wife was, in fact, having an affair with her manager. Following that, they had many discussions and arguments, which ultimately led to their splitting up.

Many people told him to divorce her and start a new family because she had said that she would never go back to him. The main reason being she was already in another relationship. Then he asked me what he should do. I was very sincere with him. I told him that the biggest contributor to this situation was himself. He had never given too much attention to her, nor did he listen to me when I told him about the dangers of her working and what it could create in their lives.

He was humble enough to recognize his mistakes and decided in his heart to not only forgive her, but to fight for her, too. It was a difficult period with many battles—fasting, praying and tears. At one point, it was necessary to send him away; the enemy had begun to put feelings of revenge in his heart.

Then, we left to São Paulo. On that trip, I told him about the importance of marriage and the need to forgive (as it could have happened to him, as well). I also reminded him of his matrimonial vows, which included "in happiness as well as in sadness" and "till death do us part." He received those words in his heart, and we continued praying for the restoration of his marriage.

Some time later, his wife confessed and repented of her sin. She received the forgiveness from them all. After the reconciliation, God sent them another baby as a gift and symbol of their new journey, with love and devotion to one another without hard feelings. Today, God has used them as powerful tools in the area of couples and family ministry.

Another supernatural experience we had was in the aisle of a medical center where my wife goes if needed. I saw a young woman coming out of the doctor's room very distressed by the bad news she had just received; her baby of three months was dead inside her womb. We approached her and asked if we could pray for her. She told me, "Yes," but she also explained that she was not following the Lord at that time.

She was actually on her way right then to go the hospital so they could perform the medical procedure to remove the fetus. I asked my wife to put her hands on her stomach and we prayed, "God, please revive this child and make a miracle in this womb." We were certain that God had done a miracle in that medical center. So we gave her our contact number to call us as soon as she could.

A few days later, my wife got a phone call from that young woman. She told her that when she arrived at the hospital, the doctor asked the nurses to do another ultrasound before she was taken to surgery. However, the doctor realized that the baby's heart was beating fast, confirming the miracle that God had done in that medical center.

Months later, my wife returned to that medical center and

asked the doctor about that young woman. She told us that the child had been born just days before. Glory to God! He is faithful! Jehovah-Rapha, the God Who heals!

God had used this last event to testify to my wife's family about what He had done in my life. It wasn't easy for me to get married. By the love of the Kingdom of Heaven and in order to save lives for Christ, I was summoned by God Himself to give testimony about what He had done for me—from my childhood traumas, abuses, rejections, my life in the homosexual world, and the healing miracle and freedom I received through Jesus. Many people believed, but many criticized me, too. I was even told that I should stop telling my story; otherwise, no woman would want to marry me with the past I'd come from. I said to that brother in the faith, "The most difficult thing, which was my healing and freedom, God had already done for me. Giving me a wife would be easy for Him."

One of my wife's aunts used to say that she wouldn't know how to react when she met me; she didn't know whether or not she would receive me with a stone or with a big piece of wood because she was so prejudice toward me. However, God had told me that He would use me in her family, so they would know that God had really changed my life.

Hérica's aunt was already forty years old when she found out she was pregnant. She rejected the pregnancy, demonstrating it by her words and attitudes. In her first ultrasound exam, she was told the fetus was deformed in the bladder, something like a tumor. This could stop the child from being able to eliminate its urine. So, after a more precise exam, it was diagnosed that the fetus had a lower urinary tract obstruction. These obstructions can be lower or higher. The low obstructions are often caused by problems in the male fetuses more than with a female fetus.

She became very distressed and depressed about the news of the health problem, and eventually, this information came to us to pray for her. Then God brought to my mind what he had told me before, and I knew this was the moment for Him to act through our lives.

When we arrived at the city where she lived, we fasted for three days and asked the Holy Spirit for guidance. Then we went to see her. In her house, we had the opportunity to tell her about what God had done in my life; I could speak in detail about everything that happened. She listened carefully to all that we said, but she was very sad about what she was going through. After we filled her heart with faith, we asked if we could pray for her. She said, "Yes." So I told her that she needed to ask God and her baby for their forgiveness. I explained to her that despite the fact that the fetus was only three months old, he/she was already able to absorb external reactions—like whether or not she accepted them or rejected them.

She prayed with us, "Lord, please forgive me for rejecting this baby." Then she prayed to her son, "My son, please forgive me for rejecting you. You are welcomed, and we love you!"

Following this, we laid our hands on her stomach and we prophesied healing in this baby's life. I also told her that whenever the doctor asked her which saint had performed this miracle, she should say, "Jesus." I told her to say that because she was catholic and faithful to many different saints.

The next day, she went to another city to do a microsurgery to try to unblock the baby's bladder. When she got to the hospital, the doctor looked at the exams and was completely aware of the severity of the situation. He said, "We will try our best to successfully complete this procedure, but before we start, you will need to do another ultrasound exam." When the doctor got the results, he was amazed. He said, "This is incredible! This is incredible! This is incredible!" He then asked her, "Which saint did you ask to heal your baby?"

She replied, "First, Jesus, but then I asked Mary, Peter ..."

The doctor interrupted her and asked, "Why so many saints? Only one was enough."

The only One Who can make miracles happen is Jesus! All the authority was given to Him on Heaven and Earth. Hallelujah!

After this event, all the members of Hérica's family began to respect me as a man of God. They also began to treat me with honor and dignity; my past was not a reason for bad jokes anymore. We must present to God any humiliation we have gone through, and God, at the right time, will exalt us. Today, Hérica's family treats me with great respect, and recently, I was invited by all to celebrate the 50-year wedding anniversary of my wife's parents.

I want to tell other miracles God had done through us during all these years we've been serving the Lord in Brazil, but I will put them in my next book named, WHEN JESUS SAYS, "YES." In this new book, I will be able to describe in detail these other miracles.

God has done many miracles, healings and transformations

in people's lives through us. We understand that God also has a purpose for this book to be translated into English. We believe that many people need to hear what Jesus is able to do in the lives of the ones who believe in His Name.

In spite of the fact that we live in a time when some people do not believe in the gospel, we still need to know that there is hope for the broken. JESUS IS OUR HOPE! My prayer is that your heart is open to the Holy Spirit to minister to your life.

May God bless you!
In the love of Christ Jesus.

To contact Jorge or Hérica personally, please email:

pr.jluis@hotmail.com
hericasimaya@gmail.com

To order more *Hope For The Broken*, visit:
http://www.creativepress.org